Dancing With Energy: Healing, Magick, and Mysticism

ISBN-13: 978-0615979038

First Edition

Acknowledgements

This book is dedicated to my mother, Mary Olson, who encouraged my love for reading and my fascination with non-ordinary reality. Unfortunately, she transitioned shortly before this work was complete. Her brief story is documented in a later chapter.

I want to thank my wife, author Jayde Frost, for editing my grammar, sentence structure and word usage. She was an endless source of inspiration and encouragement during the writing process.

I would like to acknowledge my close friend, Kevin, for editing the content and structure of this book. His vast knowledge of spirituality always gives me much to contemplate.

I want to thank my sister, Donna, for letting me borrow her books on metaphysics in my early childhood. She was always open to discussions about life's mysteries.

I also want to give special recognition to my digital artist, Hampton Lamoureaux, who created the original cover art for the book. We also utilized the talents of the following stock artists who contributed to the imagery of the cover: Georgina Gibson (Georgina-Gibson), Marcus Ranum (mjranum-stock), Heather Holderby (xkenren), Jeannie Numos (i-am-Jenius), Pauline Moss (Pauline Moss) and Sascha Duensing (Sirius-sdz). All of these gifted artists can be located at DeviantArt.

Table of Contents

Introduction

We are entering a new era of peace and harmony in the world. Although the evidence for modern day world conflict cannot be denied, many people believe in a greater purpose for this clash. Some sensitives attribute this to the Age of Aquarius, an age of spiritual enlightenment. This new age brings with it great opportunities for growth and expansion. It offers the chance for a leap in human potential and personal evolution. Currently, the stretching of our consciousness is felt by many. This change can be felt on many levels: physically, mentally, and spiritually. In this new age lies an opportunity to heal imbalances and reach higher states of consciousness.

You are about to learn about the energy known as Reiki. This book provides guidelines, along with specific techniques and suggestions for Reiki practice. My intention is to make this book beneficial to the basic practitioner, but voiced slightly more for the intermediate and advanced practitioner. On the other hand, novices should understand that they are not overhearing a private conversation. This manuscript is designed to speak to the reader with all levels of expertise.

Dancing with Energy is an overview of many areas of Reiki practice. I included sections such as magick, forming groups and service work that are not covered in traditional Reiki books. Some sections may be the subject of other works in the future so stay tuned.

If you are reading this, then you are probably a gifted healer. You are in good company. There are many like you seeking an opportunity for accelerated growth. In this new aeon, people want more from life and themselves. They sense the importance of connecting to God, nature, and the spirit world. It is a search for unity rather than division, balance instead of chaos.

"Dancing with Energy" introduces you to a therapeutic process, magical art, and a path to enlightenment. It is the way of Reiki and is invaluable to both novice and those who are adept. Reiki is accessible to all who desire spiritual growth and fulfillment. This book is also for those perceiving rapid changes within themselves and their community. It speaks to those sensitive individuals that feel a calling to serve and offer themselves.

This book is not only an introduction, but a manual of spiritual expansion. At the end of every chapter, there is a section called "Review Questions." This is a chance for to review the information on the subjects of each chapter. It also helps monitor the progression of your thinking toward the topic. I intend the work to act as a workbook in this way.

The exercises and techniques in the chapters are effective for a large number of students, but they are only suggestions to tapping into Reiki power. As with all spiritual teachings, test them for their usefulness. If they do not seem to work for you, alter the instructions and design them yourself.

Unfortunately, there is only a small amount of knowledge about this sacred path. Experiment with this natural healing and your own spiritual techniques. Reiki is not a rigid unchanging system, but rather a constantly evolving power. I invite you to experience its strength and beauty.

You will learn Reiki from a broad perspective, an eclectic mix. The blend will contain small amounts of Tibetan Reiki along with Hayashi/Takata Western Reiki.

If you are a beginner, this book will be an additional resource for you. However, you may need to do some extra research in certain areas. I intentionally did not add some material from other Reiki books. For example, I did not put the traditional Reiki hand positions. Nor did I include any visual representations of the symbols in Reiki level two and three. You can easily find this information on the internet without cost.

Why not put these aspects in the manuscript? One cannot effectively use the hand positions or the symbols unless you are attuned to the Reiki energy. If you are attuned to Reiki, then you should have access to the knowledge from your class whether taught live or by distance.

I introduce Reiki from a mystical perspective in this book. I have also included spiritual exercises for your development to enhance your practice. These exercises will be beneficial to non-attuned students as well. There is even information on Reiki magick, a valuable tool to manifest positive desires. I also added some material on forming Reiki groups and more.

We, human beings, are creatures of habit and do that which is familiar. The exercises within these pages are meant to be explored and practiced. I urge you to play with them with an open heart. They are designed to be fun and performed with a child-like attitude. Reiki energy is light, not heavy, and such playful excursions should be done with the same attitude.

Reiki opened many doors in my life and helped me traverse worlds. I also met many wonderful people who became close friends during my studies. The energy led me to new spiritual heights and consoled me during times of despair. It is a kind of invisible friend that will never go away.

Hopefully, you will find a powerful subtle force in these pages beckoning to be summoned. Reiki is the universal energy that existed before the beginning of time and consciousness. It already knows you and how to interact with your body. Are you willing to invest in the essence of healing and creative manifestation? Indulge yourself in the gift of Reiki and treasure its many gifts.

Everyone can benefit from the love and light of Reiki. It gives needed strength during the difficult times in one's life. There are people feeling physical, mental, and spiritual poverty. They have a longing for the nourishment of an unseen source. This force may be calling you. Will you answer?

I invite you to walk beside me as Reiki reveals itself in these pages. Enjoy the beginning of a deeply personal relationship with an unseen reality. If you allow it to enter within, Reiki will transform your life in many unexpected ways.

The ideas herein may challenge your current view of reality. There is no objective scientific explanation for this force. Reiki is a strangely familiar but unique mystical healing system. It is a subtle yet powerful force currently being unleashed into the world. As children of divinity, this is your birthright, which is granted by nature.

I believe that Reiki is a vocation, a calling for a greater intelligence to direct healing energy and guide one's life. If this idea appeals to you, then ask yourself the following questions: Do I desire personal change? Am I ready to be an instrument for this shift?   If the answer is "yes," then follow me along the path of Reiki.

Chapter I: The Healing Energy

I want to begin this journey into the Reiki mysteries by setting the right frame for learning. If you are interested in learning Reiki, one must adopt what is known in Zen as the "beginners mind." This means setting aside all of your preconceived ideas to enter a mental space of openness. Allow yourself the luxury to alter your beliefs temporarily. It is the ability to enter a place of infinite possibilities. You are crossing into the realms of energy and magic.

What exactly is Reiki? Quite simply, Reiki is a Japanese form of energetic healing. It is often called the Usui System of Natural Healing in the western hemisphere. The Usui system is a formulation of healing techniques developed by the master healer Mikao Usui. However, the term Reiki is not entirely accurate. Reiki refers to various systems of healing touch employing energy work around the world.

Reiki is a healing art, a form of spiritual healing. It works by uplifting us to a higher state of functioning. Often, the person experiences a spiritually renewed feeling even better than before the treatment. This is one of the positive outcomes of this form of healing.

Spiritual healing improves the condition of the body, emotions, and intellect, all of which represent one system. Many spiritual healers report an increased personal sense of vitality and empowerment during their sessions. These feelings are an inner experience of Reiki power felt from within.

Spiritual healing flows as an unseen force rather than a visible one. This invisible power originates from a universal power. The source is often described as God, Goddess, Higher Power, or Ultimate Reality. The label does not matter because this source is beyond our present understanding.

In Reiki, as in other forms of spiritual healing, the whole is greater than the sum of its parts. There is much more happening than someone laying their hands on another person. In other words, a greater action is involved than can be fully observed. This is extraordinary when you think about it. Reiki is a collaboration between the healer and the source, the creative intelligence. Some other methods of spiritual healing include prayer and meditation. These therapeutic modalities exist cross-culturally and withstood the test of time.

Reiki is a form of energetic healing that flows from the palms, eyes, and breath. It is derived from the Japanese words "Rei" and "Ki." "Rei" means spirit and "Ki" means energy. Therefore, Reiki is spiritually guided energy used to enhance health and reach one's potential. It does not involve the personal energy of the person, but instead is derived from an infinite universal energy source.

I refer to Reiki as "energy," but what exactly is energy? According to quantum physics, every bit of matter consists of energy. All physical objects both animate and inanimate consist of atoms and molecules that give it structure. Within those atoms are subatomic particles swirling at incredible speeds. Atoms consist of more than 99.9% empty space. This means that all matter is energetic by nature. Therefore, physical bodies are energy and can be affected by such.

There is a similar concept that is expanded upon by most metaphysical theories. Classical metaphysics states that the spiritual and material worlds lie along a continuum. At one end is the material world, and, the other end is the spirit realm. The physical realm is the world of the visible form as perceived by the five senses. The spiritual realms are unseen and felt through psychic senses. It is commonly thought that both exist and occupy the same space. How is this possible?

Each realm vibrates at a different rate. The spirit world moves quickly while the physical world is much slower. Also, the faster or higher the vibration, the less visible the world as well as the objects contained within it. Imagine someone holding a pencil between their thumb and forefinger. A pencil is tangible with a solid structure. If you cause it to swing back and forth or vibrate between your fingers, it becomes more difficult to observe. In fact, the instrument becomes less visible and begins to blur. It becomes more energized by your physical effort.

It is commonly understood that Reiki flows through the healer, not from the healer. This simply means that spirit allows Reiki to direct itself without depleting the energy of the healer. Many students report that they feel invigorated after the Reiki session, as it is transformed by it. This is probably the case because Reiki flows into the healer before exiting through the hands. In other words, the practitioner allows a force greater than herself to pass through the body. Reiki then balances the healer's energy centers allowing her to feel more peaceful and complete.

Chakras

It is important to understand the energy centers of the body when engaging in Reiki practice. These spiraling vortexes of energy are called chakras in East Asian thought. The term "chakra" means "wheel" in sanskrit. Chakras are unseen wheels of energy that influence us physically, psychologically, and spiritually. They affect every aspect of human experience and influence them on a daily basis. There will be a more thorough discussion of chakras in a later chapter.

Spiritual Attunements

I am often asked exactly how one channels this healing energy. This question has a surprising answer. An aspiring student must undergo a spiritual initiation, an attunement to access the power. This rite of passage is only passed from master to student. Furthermore, the actual initiation rites are taught strictly at the highest level of practice. Reiki is quite similar to many old mystery religions in these ways. These customs allow Reiki to preserve its rich mystical tradition.

Many students ask about the nature of the attunement to Reiki. The attunement process allows a human being to be in harmony with the universal energy. The outcome of this event is the capacity to channel life energy in great quantities. However, this is not a phenomenon to be taken lightly. An attunement is a permanent spiritual imprint that bestows increased personal power. The utmost responsibility should be taken with its expression.

A Reiki attunement is not a fearful event for most people. Actually, it is quite a pleasant experience. Some students even receive life-changing revelations and insights. Here is how it works: The student sits in a straight back chair with eyes closed. Master and student bow to each other before beginning the procedure. After this gesture of respect, the Reiki master makes the proper adjustments to the student's aura to allow for Reiki to flow. When the attunement is complete, the subject is forever transformed and able to channel Reiki for his entire life.

Reiki masters (the teachers) tell us that side effects are possible with attunements. This is commonly referred to as a healing crisis. It is a natural event associated with various energy therapies such as Reiki, Shiatsu, and acupressure. Toxins are released from cells into the blood stream during this time. Water is typically consumed after energy sessions or attunements to flush out these impurities.

Detoxification

The symptoms of a healing crisis result from a kind of detox. There are two forms: physical and emotional. Each form of detox traditionally occurs with a specific advancement of Reiki practice. However, everyone is different in their physical/emotional make-up. Some practitioners experience no signs of either kind, or perhaps a mixture of both. Those who are nicotine dependent or indulge in similar unhealthy habits experience more noticeable signs of detoxification.

Many reported signs of detox associated with Reiki attunements include a liquid discharge. Crying, frequent urination, sweating, sneezing, and vaginal secretions are examples of common signs of detox. If these reactions occur, they usually express themselves shortly after the attunement process. Students also occasionally report feelings of dizziness and lightheadedness. This is due to the shifting of awareness from the attunement. The physical manifestations of the detox appear to last only a few days.

Mary's Physical Detox

An example of physical detox is illustrated by the experience of a former student. Mary is a medical transcriptionist and mother of three. She experiences much stress at her job and often smokes cigarettes. Mary heard about the health benefits of Reiki, so she chose to become attuned to the Reiki energy.

Mary asked for me to teach the course on Christmas Day, a sacred time for her. After imparting the basic instructions for Reiki practice, it was time for Mary's attunement. She closed her eyes and sat straight in her chair. After three minutes into it, a peaceful look passed over her face. She later told me about feeling a release of tension in her body. She retreated into the bathroom to urinate when the attunement was over. She went three more times within an hour. This is a common example of a physical detox.

During the attunement process, massive amounts of spiritual energy flow from the master into the student. This is extremely high vibrational energy. It is commonly believed that this energy flow releases toxins stored in physical cells. These toxins must be released and excreted from the body. If you undergo an attunement, please drink several glasses of water afterwards. The water helps flush impurities out of your body.

The cleansing of the physical, emotional, and spiritual bodies are necessary to become an effective healer. The healer must be a relatively clear vessel for Reiki to pass through her, a clean instrument for divine healing. "Instrument" is the operative word in Reiki. The Reiki practitioner is, in a sense, not actually the healer and cannot accept credit for a positive outcome. She is guided by the unseen hand of the divine architect, who allows her to channel universal energy.

An emotional detox is also associated with Reiki attunements and practice. This detox is often correlated with Reiki level II. According to student reports, this is the most common and uncomfortable form of cleansing. A student may experience bouts of unprovoked anger, anxiety, and sadness. It may appear at first glance that the attunement caused psychological harm. These changes in mood are only transitory and must be worked through to completion.

John's Emotional Detox

A Reiki student of mine, John, reported the effects of his emotional detox. John is a married father of three children and a massage therapist. He struggled to support his family and suffered from intense feelings of anger. When he began learning Reiki, John revealed his personal issues to me and was interested in obtaining greater peace of mind.

John attended his level II course a few years ago. He perceived a feeling stirring within him several days after his attunement. It was anger of an extreme magnitude. He managed to control it, but the feeling was still present. Finally, the anger released him from its clutches after several weeks.

There is an easy explanation for John's experience with Reiki. Reiki can accelerate an individual's psychospiritual evolution. John's repressed psychological wounds began to surface, the source of his inner pain. It was probably the emotional pain that precipitated the anger. After speaking with John through the years, he is no longer imprisoned by his rage and quite successful in his life.

Sandy's Story

This is another example of a profound emotional detox by a former student. Sandy attended a Reiki I workshop several years ago. She started feeling pulled to learn Reiki for an unknown reason. She believed that spiritual forces led her to the course. Although Sandy was new to the metaphysical field, she had a passion for learning about Reiki.

Sandy was an excellent student and always had interesting questions for me. However, the attunement process was the focus of her interest because of its potential transformative capabilities. A startling phenomenon occurred behind her closed eyes during her attunement. She revealed repressed memories from her childhood, memories of physical abuse. Sandy became stronger by gaining enhanced insight into her current life.

The previously described experience is not uncommon among Reiki students. Reiki attunements and treatments influence people to face their shadow selves. This is the dark unconscious parts of the psyche, which includes past history. Reiki allows old issues and problems to surface in the mind. These old psychological imprints get an opportunity for reprocessing. If the student does not resist this process, the assimilation of this old material will only be mildly uncomfortable. In time, these subconscious contents become reintegrated within the person allowing them to become more psychologically whole.

Attunement Experiences

Memories are not the only variety of mental activity experienced by Reiki students. Some students report observing images of geometric figures like triangles, squares, and circles pass through their mind. An individual may also see colors during the attunement process, usually those associated with the spectrum of light. However, I believe that no expectations should exist regarding the content of our inner experience of Reiki. Everyone is different on many levels, which influences their attunement experience.

Visual stimuli are not the only manifestation of a Reiki mystical experience. Some people receive auditory experiences such as comforting sounds or guiding voices. This may be a Reiki guide trying to impart spiritual information. A student may also simply feel a sense of love or understanding during the attunement. These people feel touched by the universal spirit flowing through everything. All of these experiences are possible, and more, during a Reiki attunement session.

Notes

Review Questions

1. What is Reiki?

2. What is the literal translation of "Reiki"?

3. What is an attunement?

4. Explain the symptoms of a physical detox from an attunement?

5. What are the symptoms of an emotional detox?

Chapter 2: Initial Training (Energy Systems)

The Chakras

What exactly are chakras? Basically, the chakras are energy stations, centers of vital energy from which the life force flows. There are seven points for these centers within the human energy field. They rotate to the right or left, depending on their individual nature. Minor chakras also exist in the extremities of the hands and feet. The activation of the chakras in the hands is a common experience in Reiki practice. They are also the portals through which the Reiki symbols travel in attunements.

I gained awareness of my chakras for the first time in my early twenties. I learned about the energy centers from studying and speaking with clairvoyant friends. Clairvoyance is the ability to see beyond physical reality into the unseen world. I had no personal knowledge of chakras until I attended a group healing meditation. During the meeting, we learned how to sense the chakras using the third eye, an invisible point between the eyes. Afterwards, we gained enough awareness to actually touch them. It was not until I actually felt the swirling energy that I was convinced of the existence of chakras.

The chakras are an important area of study in Reiki practice. They are a fundamental energy system in the mind-body, not to mention a critical factor for spiritual development. These unique energy centers have different functions in our being. They are associated with specific organs and tissues, such as the endocrine system. The chakras also greatly affect and regulate our physical and mental health. Each chakra is not only associated with our mind and body, but other elements such as color and sound. This information is extremely important in treating energy imbalances with Reiki.

The seven energy centers also correlate with a specific element, the ancient constituents of nature. These are the same elements described in magick, astrology, and earth religions: air, fire, earth, water.

According to Asian Indian philosophy, there are seven chakras. These energy vortices are commonly known as the root, sacral, solar plexus, heart, throat, third eye, and crown chakras. Some New Agers speculate the existence of other chakras, but for our purposes, we will focus on the ones traditionally described in India.

The Root Chakra

The root chakra is the first energy vortex. This portal of energy is described as existing at the base of the spine or perineum. It is associated with the color red and is represented by the element of earth. This chakra provides grounding to the individual, a connection to his instinctual human side, and governs the limbic system. If you remember, in a tree, it is the root system which keeps it solid in the earth. Similarly, this chakra, both physically and energetically, forms the basis for the higher centers.

This energy center has the reputation for strictly dealing with human base desires. These animal drives include things such as eating, sleeping, copulating, protecting, acquiring, and possessing. There are also higher functions of the root chakra such as honor, loyalty, and religious passion. It is mistake to consider this energy center inferior to the higher ones. This base chakra provides the motivation for action in the physical world.

When the first chakra is imbalanced by too much energy, an individual may become obsessed with success and materialism. He might propel himself into the excessive world of sex, money, and power. This cycle often leads to addiction and results in confusion, instability, and sorrow. The opposite occurs when this center has too little energy. He usually has little confidence in his ability to exert himself in the world. This is a recipe for poor work performance, loss of motivation to establish relationships, and inability to ground himself.

The Sacral Chakra

The sacral chakra is the second energy center. It is associated with the color orange and represented by the element of water. The location of this chakra is about an inch below the navel. If you are looking from the back, it is even with the sacrum. This point is known as the Hara, the seat of original Ki, in Reiki.

This is a sacred vessel that contains the spirit of imagination and creative longings. It is also thought to embody sexual activity. It is the joyful, playful, and procreative aspects of sex that govern this center. The second chakra concerns itself with themes like innocence, fun, light-heartedness, and creativity. These are the wonderful qualities of an innocent young child, one who approaches the world with wonder.

It has been my experience that people with an active sacral center unconsciously instill comfort in those around them. They may also be artists, writers, musicians, or counselors. These people often have a light energy to them and seem to be guided by the unseen power of possibility. Their muse tells them to place faith in the universe because a positive experience is certain.

An imbalanced sacral center produces an individual to use his creativity to manipulate people. As a consequence, grandiosity and arrogance increase within him. In addition, he becomes self-centered and materialistic, willing to bend others to his will. This ultimately leads to dissatisfaction because eventually, the manipulator becomes entangled in the web of his creation.

Another consequence of a sacral imbalance is fear. If the energy does not flow well, anxiety may result. This, in turn, creates fear of people and situations. Creativity and security are blocked from maturing. This blockage often results in avoidance and seclusion from the world.

The Solar Plexus Chakra

Next in the sequence of energy centers is the solar plexus chakra. It is responsible for maintaining your sense of self, including your ego and who you are becoming. The solar plexus chakra is associated with the color yellow. This indicates that the sphere contributes to the mental faculty of reason and logic for evaluating matters. The solar plexus center is also symbolized by the element of fire. This element is projective in nature much like the personality. Our personality is an outward expression of the inner workings of the mind.

This particular energy sphere governs emotions, even those often judged as negative. As an example, fear is often felt within the stomach area. Have you ever heard of people feeling "butterflies" in their stomach before a performance? Nervousness is the culprit on such occasions. This is also evident in the progression of illness, like ulcers. Some ulcers are exacerbated by symptoms of stress, which is a more socially acceptable term for fear. It is almost as if repressed fear is eating a person away from the inside.

The solar plexus gives us the ability to intuitively perceive impressions from our environment. My mother used to tell me, "Mark, I have a feeling in my gut about this." She was usually correct about her psychic impressions. You can be as well by learning to clear the solar plexus and open it at will.

The Heart Chakra

The heart center is the fourth center on the journey through the chakra system. This chakra rules the lungs, thymus, pericardium, and heart, all of which are located in the chest cavity. Green is the color of the heart chakra, sometimes with a hint of gold or pink. Its traditional element is that of air. This particular chakra is known to reason through the lens of the heart, to feel rather than think.

Emotional intelligence is the key phrase with this energy center. The heart chakra determines the level of vulnerability and sensitivity that we project to others. If someone refers to you as guarded, protected, or closed off, you might consider checking your heart chakra. People sometimes build walls around themselves to prevent others from getting too close. Perhaps they have been wounded and wish to prevent further psychological pain. A prolonged cycle of emotional distancing can perpetuate feelings of loneliness and sorrow. It is healthy to have boundaries, but when boundaries are excessively rigid, they can insulate us from those that we love.

The Throat Chakra

The fifth chakra is commonly known as the throat center. Light blue is the natural color associated with this energy wheel. However, various shades of blue are seen at different times. The organ ruled by this chakra is the thyroid gland. This component of the endocrine system regulates energy, temperature, and metabolism. Similarly, this center metabolizes the energy from various chakras to form our unique form of personal expression.

The key word here is "expression." The way in which we communicate is a throat-centered matter. Often, this issue manifests in one of two different ways. Either someone excessively speaks their mind or they are unable to communicate their opinion. Either of these signs indicates an imbalance in the throat area.

I've often noticed that more men typically have an energy disruption in the throat than women. I think that this results from past environmental programming that men are "doers" rather than "feelers." A man is told that he should restrict the communication of his feelings, especially fear and sorrow because those can be interpreted as weakness.

Each of us has a unique truth to express. The expression of verbal truth is important and has significant power. In some Christian groups, the "power of the spoken word" is the descriptive term for this expression. Most people agree that the mind and heart direct human action and energy, especially in speech. Therefore, an imbalance in the throat region can adversely affect a person's success in life.

The Third Eye Chakra

The sixth energy center is known as the third eye, located at the point just above the bridge of the nose between the eyes. Indigo is the color associated with this chakra. The organs connected to this point include the pituitary gland and the hypothalamus. This chakra governs all forms of mental activity including logical reasoning, abstract thinking, and fantasy. It is also the center for the psychic ability of clairvoyance.

This energy sphere allows an individual to see into the unseen world. Quite simply, a person with a well-developed third eye can observe spirit entities traveling among the living. In addition, a strong sixth chakra is extremely helpful in assessing for energy imbalances. The sensitive practitioner can observe the aura and chakras to determine their level of wellness.

Imbalance in the third eye manifests itself in different forms. Sometimes a person has difficulty seeing into the immediate future. He is unable to look forward and foresee likely outcomes from present conditions. The life patterns are indiscernible to him and become hidden from his awareness.

The Crown Chakra

The last energy center is known as the crown chakra. This sphere is at the top of the head. Traditional metaphysical thought associates it with the color violet. The pineal gland near the base of the brain is ruled by the crown chakra. This gland, like the pituitary, is a component of the endocrine system and secretes hormones to regulate body functioning.

The crown chakra is an important center for attaining higher states of awareness. It is the gateway to the higher spiritual realms of existence. Through the crown center, a human being can connect to divinity, a passageway to inspiration and spiritual communication. An individual with a healthy crown sphere (and other balanced chakras) feels an inner sense of unity with one's personal experience of the cosmos.

It is also possible for people to experience an undercharged crown center. At these times, feelings of loneliness, alienation, and sadness are noticeable. When experiencing these feelings, an individual may isolate himself from loved ones. The opposite is also true. A person may become needy and cling to people, allowing himself to become dependent on someone, replacing them as a god figure. However, it is never a healthy substitution for no mortal relationship can replace a spiritual connection with the divine.

The chakras draw energy from the surrounding environment and assimilate it into the body. This pulling helps strengthen the energy source when depleted. This is also known as "psychic vampirism." These dynamic pools of energy also project outward, giving up their life force. For example, if you ever felt drained after meeting with a needy friend, there was most likely an energy exchange between the two of you. The friend probably drew energy from your chakras. In turn, as a concerned friend, you may have willingly pushed some vital energy in their direction.

It has been my experience that chakras are capable of self-protection. Have you ever encountered a new acquaintance with whom you felt uncomfortable? If so, you probably felt a tightening in your chest or stomach. This feeling is an adjustment in life force flowing through that particular energy center. As a result, the sphere's bright light dims and restricts both incoming and outgoing energy which is a natural protective measure.

Exercise I

Here is an exercise to experience the chakras. First, be sure the lights are either dimmed or completely out. You may burn some candles to encourage this lighting. It is also permissible to burn your favorite incense. If you are uncertain about the particular choice, cinnamon is excellent because of its reputation for heightening psychic perception. Now, take several slow, deep cleansing breaths. Expand and contract your stomach during the process. Do this about ten times.

Imagine yourself completely relaxing and releasing all tension in your muscles. When you feel moderately relaxed, imagine the following colors in the indicated sequence. See the colored number in this exact order:

RED-7, ORANGE-6, YELLOW-5, GREEN-4, BLUE-3, INDIGO-2, VIOLET-1.

At this point, sense the energy within your third eye growing and expanding. The next step is to imagine a representation of your physical body in front of you. If your third eye is open, you should see the wheels of energy in the imagined form. Look at them closely. Are they bright or dim? Do you observe any cloudiness or darkness? What are their colors? Are they spinning? If so, what directions are they twirling?

If you have difficulty seeing the centers, do not become discouraged. Here are two pieces of advice. One, practice the technique for a couple of weeks. During this time, the perceptual clarity should improve remarkably. Next, some people perceive psychic information through non-visual means. If this applies to you, try to feel or hear the centers. In addition, there are many books on chakra development and perception. Expand your reading collection by indulging in these works and find the ones which work best for you.

Exercise II

This exercise begins after the relaxation of your physical body. At this point, rub your hands together enough to produce heat-inducing friction. This action activates minor chakras, allowing increased sensitivity in this area. You may even feel a tingling sensation in the hands. This is a natural consequence of chakra excitation on the skin's surface.

Use your non-dominant hand (receptive) to scan the front of your body. For example, if you are right-handed, move your left hand, palm inward, up and down your body. The opposite is true if you are left-handed. Be sure that the hand is about two to four inches away from the skin. After scanning the body, you may sense small collections of energy. If you do, then congratulations! These are the chakras. If you do not sense anything, clear your mind of all expectations regarding the experience. Rub your hands together once again and continue with the procedure. If there is no success, try again at a later time.

The energy centers are excellent indicators of mind-body health. Every influence from our environment affects them whether it is an abusive co-worker or an oncoming cold. In other words, the chakras respond to the thoughts, intentions, and feeling states of others. Chakras respond not only energetically speaking, but also to the interpretation of another's actions. For example, the threat of a verbally abusive boss may influence the heart chakra to restrict its energy flow. This protective measure allows the person to function at work with an unfriendly host.

Bodily illness can also either disrupt or result from chakra activity. Often, our defenses become strained through environmental stress. This allows us to be vulnerable to unhealthy outside influences in our environment. The body then loses its ability to defend against viruses and various other microorganisms. The outcome is physical illness.

The Aura

Philosophers and holy men have speculated about the existence of a radiance along the contours of the body. This is also reflected in common conversation among individuals. In modern society, people are said to have a "pleasant aura" or a "peaceful aura." What exactly is this thing? The aura is a bioelectric energy field that surrounds all living beings. An aura is an invisible boundary that borders the physical body. It offers protection from harmful unseen influences, like energetic skin. This protection is limited by its strength, and the condition of this field is determined by our thoughts, feelings, and health.

Thoughts are a natural part of the human mind. We constantly process information through our senses and assign meaning to those experiences. All to often, our minds direct us towards self-defeating thoughts and behaviors. This creates feelings of loneliness, inadequacy, anger, sadness, and fear. These feelings often lead to a weakening of the auric field. Our defenses are compromised by an inner enemy: ourselves.

Stress is a natural part of functioning and participating on planet Earth. There are two kinds of stress: eustress and distress. Eustress, the good stress, is actually useful because it helps us focus on solving problems. Distress, the bad stress, heightens physiological arousal such as heart rate and blood pressure. If this becomes chronic psychological stress, then it can be overwhelming and harmful to our body. Clairvoyants have noticed that persistent stress creates tears in the aura. It is believed that these energy abrasions can also be seen in Kirlian photographic images of the aura.

Auric Layers

There are seven traditional layers of the auric field. Those who have either inborn or developed clairvoyant sight can view these energy patterns. The etheric body is the one closest to the body and is easiest to see. It is indicative of your physical health. The emotional body is the second layer and shows emotional wellness. Next, the third layer is the mental layer. This consists of the intellect, beliefs, and consciousness, a human's mental health. The fourth layer is the astral layer, the medium through which we travel to the spiritual realms. A map of our physical bodies and their energy disruptions is the sixth layer, the etheric template. The sixth auric layer is the celestial body, the vehicle for spiritual ecstasy. Finally, the seventh layer is the ketheric template. It is connected to the crown chakra and the one most difficult to see. If you want to see wonderful visual representations of the aura, treat yourself to the work of visionary artist Alex Grey.

Karma

Karma will be discussed as a major concept in healing in a future chapter. It can also be a major determinant of overall wellness and strength in the aura. This makes sense because karma is about establishing balance within oneself. It is through the exposure to many different life experiences that a human progresses on his or her path to enlightenment. True wisdom develops through many lifetimes as you face your personal spiritual challenges.

Humans are thought to retain karmic influences from previous incarnations. These unresolved forces seek expression to teach us lessons while we embody a physical form. Many illnesses can result from this life or even much farther back in time. It is no wonder that some maladies develop quickly and linger with persistence. These energetic determinants of serious illness can build momentum through many lifetimes. As a result, many sessions may be required to successfully improve the problem.

The Origin of Illness

Throughout the ages, philosophers and wise men speculated about the cause of illness and disease. Modern medicine offers scientific theories to this perennial debate. Contemporary research in the fields of genetics, biology, and chemistry theorize physical explanations for all physical disorders. Microorganisms such as viruses, bacteria, and renegade cells are often blamed. This interpretation does not satisfy most healers. What about alternate explanations for these ailments? Are medical scientists looking at the causes or simply viewing the effects? These are important thoughts to ponder.

Based on my observations, most physical illness is associated with a prior energetic imbalance. This means that a dysfunction in an energy system occurred before the bodily symptoms of the disease itself.

This is not a popular view among physicians trained in modern day medicine. Medical doctors believe in the visible world of microbes seen through the lens of a powerful microscope. They are thought to be the culprits of poor health and waning wellness. Still, an unseen penetrating reality exists that forewarns an impending ailment. This invisible existence is the vast world of the meridian, aura, and chakra energy systems.

Meridians

I mentioned the chakra and aura systems in regard to Reiki healing. There is one more important energy matrix to discuss, the meridians. The chakras are energy centers and the aura is an energy field. The meridians are different in that they are energy pathways. These invisible paths are similar to the arteries inside the body, except they carry subtle energy.

Meridians travel in lines through all of the major organs of the body. There are twelve such pathways that flow near the surface of the skin. They also affect the function of all organs in which they cross. Therefore, the meridians greatly influence our mental and physical wellness.

These energy channels work well only when they flow free and unimpeded. Whenever such tributaries become blocked, illness and disease can result. Energy workers can easily assess the meridians objectively by applying muscle testing procedures. If you have well developed psychic abilities, then the imbalances can be intuited. At this point, a Reiki practitioner can correct the blockage and return the energy system to homeostasis.

Chi or ki is the life force that empowers all living beings with vitality. Yin and Yang are the components of this universal energy. How do they relate to the body? If the energy system has excessive yang, then the system can be over stimulated. On the other hand, if there is excessive yin present, then the organs are sluggish. Optimal health occurs when both yin and yang are in harmony and balanced. Whenever these tributaries become blocked, illness and disease can result.

The twelve primary meridians channel chi through the following organs: large intestine, small intestine, bladder, spleen, pericardium or circulation-sex, gall bladder, kidney, liver, heart, lungs, triple warmer, and stomach. Meridians also interact with other systems for the circulation of chi. The secondary meridians do not correlate to specific organs.

A successful Reiki session can balance the yin and yang in the body. Reiki can also dissolve any blockages in the meridians and facilitate a smooth flow of Chi.

The Microcosmic Orbit

The microcosmic orbit is an energy exercise practiced in Chi Gung. It is often included in Reiki level III material and can be performed by non-Reiki practitioners. The practitioner circulates Chi through their body through two meridians, the governing and conception vessels. Breath and intention direct the energy through these pathways.

Students who regularly practice the microcosmic orbit report increased energy and vitality. It is also reputed to cleanse the mind and body of impurities. Taoist masters are believed to use such exercises to increase longevity and live indefinitely. If you want to try the microcosmic orbit, it is included at the end of this chapter.

Emotional Sources of Disease

There are many factors that lead to a diseased mind and body. Genetics, nutrition, environmental conditions, and activity level are just a few. Human emotions also play an important role in determining our degree of wellness. As an example, negative emotions resonate with specific organs and particular illnesses. This section lists the common relationships between our feelings and the major diseases of the body. Understand that these are noted correlations and not necessarily indications of causation.

Eyes- A wise philosopher once said that the eyes are the windows to the soul. This is often true, but for other reasons as well. The eyes are one of the keys to our awareness of the world. If our vision is broad, we see life with clarity, depth, and perspective. A limited vision is usually obscured by rigidity and inflexibility. The most common vision impairment is near and farsightedness. Both near and farsighted people have different problems with the same theme: What are you trying to avoid seeing?

Nearsightedness is simply the ability to see up close, but not at a distance. This malady is associated with being unwilling to look into the future, a fear of life. Farsightedness is marked by the resistance to being fully present in the moment. The stereotypical dreamer or absentminded professor fall into this category.

Kidneys- the kidneys primary function is to cleanse the blood of harmful waste products. These impurities are collected in the bladder before its final release. This is the first symbolic function of the kidneys: the release of the destructive. The kidneys are also physically connected to the adrenal glands, the producer of the fight or flight response and the hormone, adrenaline. In this way, kidney disturbances are associated with the harboring of fear. This means the fear of loss, fear of expression, and fear of death.

Legs- The legs are the basic supporters of our upper body. They keep our balance as we walk through the world. Legs transport us through our physical journeys through life and fail us during stressful circumstances. Our loved ones preface bad news by saying "You better sit down." People overwhelmed by another's beauty say, "He or she made me weak in the knees."

Liver- The liver is the organ that detoxifies the impurities from our digestive system. These bodily poisons can cause sickness and death if unchecked. According to Chinese medicine, the liver also filters the anger from our bloodstream and stores it within its own tissue. This process keeps us in a relatively balanced state. Anger and resentment are natural in modest quantities and short duration. However, excessive anger stored over a long period of time can strain the liver unless released.

Heart- The heart is a muscle made of soft tissue in our chest. This organ circulates blood and emotional energy. It is a symbol for emotional and spiritual love, and all the accompanying pain. Romantic love or eros draws us toward our desire. Spiritual love or "agape" helps us see the fullness of our partner. Both are the hearts striving for connection and fulfillment.

People often experience grief due to a major loss in their life. They are said to be "broken hearted" or having "lost heart." Heart conditions are signs that this center is unbalanced, a block in experiencing love or simply difficulty expressing it. The basic message is to be still, and find that loving place within you. Learn to love yourself unconditionally and share that love with other people.

Lungs- the lungs circulate life force through our breathing. Unfortunately death is imminent at the end of breath. This concept extends through many different cultures. Chi or Ki is known as "vital force" or breath in eastern religions. Breath or spirit was also blown into Adam from the mouth of God. Breath represents the animating force within all living beings.

Fear often creates shallow breathing, especially in a life threatening situation. Breaths that are slow and deep are relaxing and empowering. Deep breathing allows us to feel comfortable and fully involved in life. The spiritual master is at ease with himself and the world. On the other hand, breathlessness is often a symbolic rejection of life, a denial of its terms. Be mindful of deep issues concerning fear and anxiety with lung conditions. These feelings should be addressed with the gentle touch of Reiki.

Lung conditions, like asthma, may show a difficulty in adapting to a changing life situation. Coughing can indicate the suppression of deep seated feelings, and a need to express them. In other words, an unwillingness to adapt to new conditions nor release our pent up emotions. These themes are both troubling and can be resolved with Reiki energy.

Feet- The feet are my favorite part of the body/mind system. They are filled with much information. Your meet are maps to your chakras and other energy systems. This is a major reason for Reiki self-healing on the feet.

The feet are also a map of all the internal organs written on your soles. Reflexology states that health can be improved by pressing specific points on the feet. A number of massage therapists have alerted me about my current physical conditions just by touching my feet. I am grateful to reflexology for its ability to diagnose my stomach problems like chronic indigestion. This information helped me create important life style changes.

A well trained reflexologist can stimulate digestion, release tension, and increase healing in every system in the body. A Reiki therapist can, likewise, set the stage for recovery by attending to the feet.

The feet connect us with the physical world. Have you ever heard the phrase, "He has both feet firmly on the ground?" This may mean that they are "down to earth."In other words, feet allow us to be grounded to life, especially in an emotional context.

Are you mentally grounded during your daily activities? Some people are said to have their "head in the clouds." Artists, writers, and other creative people unfairly obtain this label. The feet symbolically remind us to care for ourselves. We must remember to socialize, eat, and sleep in adequate amounts.

One final thought regarding the feet. Reiki lore suggests that Ki is drawn from above and below: Heavenly and Earth Ki. The earthly Ki enters our being from the bottom of our feet. It circulates through us before exiting the hands during a Reiki session.

Sex Organs-The entirety of our sex organs are connected to procreation and sexuality. They give us our identity as male and female. Therefore, the sex organs are strongly linked to our deep personal issues of masculinity and femininity.

Problems with the sex organs often indicate an inner struggle. This can be a difficulty in sharing, trusting, or experiencing comfort with your partner. Problems such as frigidity, and impotence can mark unresolved pain: guilt, insecurity, and shame.

Many mystical traditions, including tantra, believe that sexual energy is divine. This energy creates partnerships and connections on the physical level. Sex also can be abused and overindulged. Sexually transmitted diseases can result from improper use of sexual enjoyment. On the other hand, sexual energy promotes life, passion, and new beginnings. Is it not interesting that the most profane phrase points to an action that brings forth new life?

Back- Where is the most common pain experienced by adults in the United States? The back. How many people complain of a "bad back?" This is usually reported by males. They may even tell you about an old football injury or other such war story.

The back has traditionally been a storage place for all the experiences that cause us pain and confusion. These feelings accumulate and cause structural weakness in areas. As an example, betrayal is marked by the phrase: "She stabbed me in the back." Another example is the teenager who feels burdened by his father's expectations, "Get off my back."

Exercise I: The Microcosmic Orbit

1. Sit down in a comfortable position.

2. Place tongue at roof of the mouth. This connects the governing and conception vessels (secondary meridians).

3. Contract the Hui Yin point. This is the area between your genitals and anus. Hold for the entire exercise.

3. You must breathe abdominally for the microcosmic orbit. As you inhale, your stomach should expand. As you exhale, your stomach should contract.

4. As you breathe in, imagine the chi energy dropping from your tan tien/hara (2 inches below your belly button) to the base of your spine. Allow the energy to rise up the center line of your back into your crown.

5. As you exhale, allow the energy to descend the midline down the front of the body into the tan tien.

6. Repeat four and five until you intuitively know to stop.

Review Questions

1. What is a chakra? Name all seven.

2. What is an aura?

3. What is the definition of a meridian?

4. What is a possible origin of physical illness?

5. Name three body parts and the emotional connections associated with them.

6. What are the benefits of practicing the microcosmic orbit?

Notes

Ch. 3: The Beginning

Reiki I is the first step along this wonderful healing path. If you are new to Reiki, then you are in for a delightful experience. Reiki tends to give people exactly what they need to maintain their balance. This is a missing element in many people's lives. All human beings seek to excel in some area of life in their own way. However, many people choose the wrong means to provide lasting satisfaction.

The goal to living a fulfilling life is harmony according to many spiritual traditions. This simply means the mind and body working together with minimal conflict. Reiki teaches us to live in serenity, peace, and harmony with all beings, including ourselves.

Self-Healing

Healing ourselves is the first step to truly becoming powerful Reiki therapists. This does not mean that you have to be perfect to practice Reiki. Far from it, but it does mean that you need to be fairly balanced for this work. This is especially true for leading individual sessions and conducting workshops.

I mention self-healing because Reiki I probably marks the beginning of your quest as a healer. How does one become more balanced? The answer to this question is based upon your own individual needs and desires. One option for students is to undergo psychotherapy to explore unresolved emotional issues. Counseling can be helpful for many reasons. Everyone needs another person to really listen and help them work through their blind spots. I saw a therapist to work through some personal problems several years ago. It was a wonderful experience that I will always remember. The best part is the improvement in all my healing work. I no longer had many of those dark filters through which I saw the world.

Psychology has a rich tradition of making students undergo analysis. In the early days of psychotherapy, schools required students to undergo therapy with a professional psychoanalyst. This helped minimize any unhealthy filters with which the student brought to his clients. I believe that a similar program would be helpful for Reiki students.

It is advisable to experience a Reiki session from a trained Usui healing master, but not entirely necessary. You have both the power and ability to balance yourself with the energy. This is a divine gift that lasts throughout your entire life. A common belief among Reiki practitioners is that regular self-healing sessions lead to greater longevity and slows aging. Perhaps it is not a coincidence that avid Reiki self-healers appear younger than their age.

Few students ever take advantage of this valuable strategy for self-transformation. I hear many rationalizations for this neglected practice. The most popular is, "I don't have enough time to practice on myself." Another excuse is, "I'm unable to balance myself with the energy." These ideas are myths that will prevent you from fully participating in the world of Reiki.

Some people complain that they are too busy to practice Reiki. Other practitioners say that they are preoccupied with work, family, and other obligations. There is simply not enough time! If you think about it, few things exist in this universe in equal quantities. Everyone has different amounts of wealth, strength, and education. All people are given twenty-four hours in a day. No one receives any less than their friends, neighbors, or politicians. It is untrue that no time exists for self-care. It is true that healing yourself is not a priority sometimes.

Developing a consistent self-healing practice can actually save time. I become more efficient in all my activities when I apply Reiki to myself. Every task in which I engage in has more quality, focus, and speed. Are you not worth investing the extra time for self-care?

One important key to becoming an extraordinary Reiki healer is integrating the practices in your daily life. This does not require much time and energy. Ask yourself what times during the day that you can practice. Consider times during the work day. Do you receive coffee breaks and lunches? If Reiki is consistently used daily, ten or fifteen minutes is all that is necessary for spiritual balance.

I perform the Usui system daily on myself for greater energy and peace of mind. This sixteen year habit changed my life drastically helping me to live with more peace and vitality. Also, I learned to integrate Reiki in my life by practicing each day. As an example, I perform Reiki in the morning, before work, as part of my energy ritual. This is an energizing and wonderful way to begin the day.

Mike, a student of mine, has a slightly different routine. He sends Reiki to himself fifteen minutes before going to bed. This helps him release tension and have pleasant dreams. Mike's claims are not unusual because Reiki is known to promote sleep in the restless.

A common excuse is that treating oneself with Reiki is impossible. If Reiki flows through the palms, why should you be unable to do this to yourself? There are only two requirements to be successful in treating oneself. Patience and sensitivity to your body are vitally important. It also may take a few minutes to notice a positive change upon touching your body.

Students often stop self-healing sessions too soon because it is not instantly gratifying. It is a human tendency to seek maximum results in the least amount of time. However, Reiki cannot be hurried. If you are physically ill, it will usually take longer to feel a beneficial effect. My intuition is that the energy travels to the disturbed area before exiting the hands. This means the palms may not change temperature until much later. Temperature change is a common sign of Reiki activation.

One of the reasons that I emphasize self-healing to my students is the issue of self-care. Energy healers are more likely to worry about other people's imbalances than their own. This is not beneficial in the long term. It also does not help due to the stress that we face on a daily basis. A fast-paced life brings chronic stress and increased responsibility.

Healing Others

You probably noticed that I did not talk about Reiki healing for others yet. Through the self-care of regular Reiki treatments, you first learn about helping others. For example, a common staple in many Reiki books are the traditional hand positions. They are valuable for the sake of history and tradition. However, one should ultimately place their hands according to the direction of their own internal guidance. I imagine the traditional hand placements like the training wheels of a bicycle. Once you gain your balance through practice, they no longer become a necessity.

Practicing Reiki on others requires a stable and comfortable surface. I recommend investing in a massage table for comfort and maneuverability. A sofa is more comfortable than a table for the client, but not the practitioner. The healer would likely have to kneel to reach the entire body. A bed may be even more comfortable than the sofa, but it still may not be the proper height or have the easy access to all sides.

Removing Disturbed Energy

We have explored Reiki as a powerful healing system. As a review, the student channels spiritual energy into people in need. This aids the body in restoring its natural harmony. However, adding healing power is only one aspect of Reiki practice. Removing negative energy is equally crucial to effective healing.

Removing malefic energy is a major part of many healing traditions. Native American, African, and Polynesian shamans use similar techniques in their spiritual practice. These customs later became popular among the early Reiki practitioners. This method is used to promote the healing of physical, emotional, and spiritual disorders. Some people use it to remove blocks in certain areas of their life. This technique can also unblock prosperity, love, and career problems.

Some students ask, "Why remove energy from an already unbalanced system?" Negative energy contributes to a dysfunctional mind and body. It prevents the organs and systems from optimal functioning. Who does not want maximum energy and vitality? Of course, the force may transform the malefic energy by simply adding Reiki over time. Unfortunately, this method of Reiki treatment is much more time consuming. Let's discuss Ki energy before going any further in energy treatment.

Ki

There are two kinds of Ki in the human body, positive Ki and negative Ki. Reiki circulates positive Ki. Negative Ki arises from emotions of anger, jealousy, sadness, and fear. These feelings can all be reduced to the latter such as the fear of loss or unmet expectations. Ki is also generated from our inner mental activity. For example, thoughts of violence and sickness transform plus Ki to minus Ki. On the other hand, love, hope, and inspiration enhance the positive Ki in the body.

This works according to the universal law of attraction. That is, thoughts attract ideas of a similar nature due to magnetic resonance. Have you ever felt loving feelings while in a good mood? It is easy to maintain this pattern with enough momentum. Similarly, a series of minus thoughts can break the psychological rhythm and attract unsavory contemplations. This new tone shifts the quality of Ki in another direction.

I do not want readers to confuse plus or minus Ki with the labels of good and bad. The latter terms are value judgments. Words like positive and negative refer to overall quality. A car battery is a helpful metaphor. It has positive and negative plates to carry an electrical charge. Both are necessary to power the battery and start the engine. Would it not be funny to refer to the good and evil parts of a battery?

Negative Ki often leads to illness. Sickness is not necessarily bad or evil. Some people may need their illness to learn a spiritual lesson. They may be learning compassion and humility or simply taking advantage of a karmic opportunity. Perhaps the infirmed are paving the way to greater long term health through their sickness. It is wise to consider these possibilities before releasing your healing ability.

Negative Ki works by collecting around physical organs such as the heart, kidney, and liver. The organs are not only affected by this energy. The chakras and meridians are also impacted. In fact, the energy often forms a shape that can be psychically perceived. One can work with the shape and image to transform its negative influence.

The Techniques

How exactly do you remove negative energy from someone? First, set your intention by calling in your healing guides. Ask for their help in removing malefic energy to promote the client's health. Invite the client to also call upon their healing guides, masters, or higher power(s) for assistance. Finally, draw the first three Reiki symbols in your palms: distance, power, and mental. It is now time to begin with your Reiki friends present.

There are many metaphysical techniques for ridding oneself of impurities from the aura. Here is one method for releasing negative energy from the energy systems.

Shamanic Excision

1. Take a deep breath. Ask the client to say his name three times. Focus upon any first impressions regarding their personality and habits.

2. Encourage the client to speak about the condition needing healing. Listen carefully to his words. As you listen, hold one part of your mind back to psychically perceive the condition needing care. Write down any impressions, no matter how faint or fleeting.

3. Ask him to close their eyes and reflect upon the problematic issue. Tell him: "If this issue were in your body, where would it be? The client should not have any difficulty choosing the area. Tension or pain will give them a sure sign.

4. Tell him to see the area in detail. Ask him: If this issue had an appearance, how would it look? If they can envision the problem, then inquire for more information.

5. Ask them several more questions: What is its color, shape, and texture? Does it speak or make a sound? If so, what does it sound like?

6. If he clearly answers these questions, tell him that you both will work together to release this energy.

7. Stand over your client. Redraw the power symbol on your palms. Imagine your hands filling with light and growing more magnetic. See thin beams of light expand from the tips of your fingers; they should extend several inches. Take your receiving hand (the opposite of your dominant hand), and move it close to the afflicted part.

8. Begin to pull the "energy goo" out of the area. Inhale as you draw the malefic energy away from the body.

9. Now turn away from your client. Exhale and release the energy into the earth with a downward motion. Be sure not to release the energy toward anyone standing nearby. This caveat only applies during a demonstration or Reiki share. It is unlikely a third party will be sitting in on a private session.

10. The last technique is to imagine that you are a Karate master. Forcefully, use the knife edge of your hand to cut the air between you. This last effort breaks the energetic bond.

This procedure may take less than thirty seconds. However, a serious blockage can take twenty minutes. Trust your intuition to decide when to stop. Also, consider that the client may need several sessions to completely release the energy.

Good work! You now have a basic understanding of the second half of Reiki healing. This technique is especially helpful for people who resist tough therapies. You can pull out the malefic energy without touching the client.

Blessing Food

We are taught as children to always say grace before eating dinner. This custom is especially important during the meal at Thanksgiving. The prayer of gratitude is sometimes even referred to as "the blessing." In other contexts, Catholic priests bless the host before being consumed by church members during mass. Reiki can not only be used to heal and restore, but also to bless the food, a magical act in itself.

The blessing increases the vibration of the food before consuming it. Many claim that the blessing makes the food more nourishing and palatable. Others assert that the rite transforms itat an essential level making the food more easily assimilated by the body. A meal that is electrified with universal energy brings more vitality and exuberance. Are you ready to take dinner to a more wonderful level?

There are many variations to the ritual of blessing food with Reiki energy. I prefer this version:

Begin with your hands in a prayer position at the heart level. You may also take a few calming deep breaths to become centered. Celebrate your ability to acquire the resources to buy or prepare the meal. Feel gratitude to the universe for supporting you in this quest. Next, set your intention silently within your mind or verbally to empower the food with life enhancing energy. Next, rub your palms together to activate the chakras in your hands. Place both hands over the meal (chips and cookies included). Allow the Reiki energy to flow; it may take a minute. Charging food generally requires less time than charging a human being with vitality. Look inward toward your intuitive guidance to decide when to stop the process. The food will not tell you. Finally, consume the meal with peace and the spirit of joy.

Exercise I: Self-Healing

Applying Reiki to yourself can be both simple and fun. I will show you a simple strategy to heal your own body in a moment. First, remember to take several slow, deep breaths. I use a Prana Yoga breathing sequence wherein I breathe in for a specific count, hold it for two, and breathe out for double the inhalation. For example, you may breathe in for four counts, hold for two, and exhale for eight. My current breathing routine is six, two, and twelve.

Breathing slowly calms the mind and body, a useful technique in today's fast-paced society. Before I give you a simple technique for this purpose, remember to sit in a location with minimal noise.

Begin by sitting or lying down in a comfortable position. Decide on the number of counts for your yoga breathing exercise. Take in a slow, deep breath. Now hold it. Exhale slowly. Do this seven times. Focus on your feet.

This is the location that I use for all Reiki treatments. According to reflexology, the feet are a pathway to every major organ and energy system. By initially working with the feet, you allow Reiki to begin removing energy blockages before actually treating specific areas. Let the energy travel into the feet until you feel it is time to stop. If you have difficulty trusting your intuition, designate a specific time to cease healing a location, such as five minutes. You may keep a wrist watch with a timer on it or observe a clock to do this.

Proceed to place your hands on your knees, one hand at a time. It is important not to break contact with the body even for an instant. This stops the energy circuit. When the time is right, move your hands to the chakra centers. Chakras cover the flowing areas: genitals, sacrum, solar plexus (upper stomach), heart, throat, forehead, and crown.

After you finish working those body areas, devote attention to any places that carry discomfort. Place your hands at these points. Know that the universal spirit will provide healing to your body. Finally, open your eyes and take several deep breaths. Congratulate yourself for finishing your first self-healing session.

At this point, notice how you feel physically and mentally. Some beginning Reiki students are not accustomed to the Reiki energy. They sometimes feel light headed and ungrounded after a session. If this happens, do something to center yourself like eating a hearty meal. Listening to music also works well.

Exercise II: Reiki Facial

The following routine is a popular exercise among female Reiki practitioners. A student of mine calls it "The Reiki Facial." Basically, this is a concentration of healing energy into the facial muscles. After only a few sessions, the face develops a more youthful glow. This makes sense because Reiki tends to improve blood circulation. Poor blood flow to the facial muscles can lead to wrinkles.

Begin the session by rubbing your hands together and set the intention to beautiful the face. Place each hand with the palms and fingers extended over the eyes. Let the healing energy flow into them. As the hands are kept in place, feel the eyes relax and release tension in the surrounding muscles. Now, move your left and right palm over each side of the face. Keep the hands about half an inch from the skin. You may feel heat on surface of you face. Move your hands over the surface of the face as guided by your intuition. As you move your hands, the Reiki energy relaxes the muscles in the face. It helps your skin become healthier. As you continue gliding your hands, know that you are becoming more physically beautiful. Your inner beauty is being unleashing into your physical form.

We will now finish this session with the rest of the head positions. Now, place both hands over the ears. Some students report greater sensitivity in their hearing after working with this area. After the ears receive the necessary attention, place your hands on each side of the head. This position balances both hemispheres of the brain, the left (logical) and the right (intuitive). After your intuition gives the message to move, place your hands on the crown of the head. This position opens your God center and strengthens the connection between you and the divine.

Exercise 3: Reiki Ball

Here is the first exercise to offer a preview into the art of Reiki Magick. As a first degree Reiki practitioner, you have the ability to direct energy according to your will. The first direction learned is to wield Reiki into another person to restore their harmony and well being. A second direction is toward yourself for your own energetic balance. You are now ready to learn a basic technique for manifesting your desires.

Sit in a comfortable position with your back straight and spine properly aligned. Inhale a few slow deep breaths for relaxation and focus. Exhale any lingering tension. Feel itflow downward and exit the bottoms of your feet. Hold both your hands together at eye level.They should be mirroring each other, like holding an imaginary soft ball. Continue rhythmic breathing and allow the energy to collect between your palms.

Move your hands slowly over the Reiki energy to the top, bottom, and sides. Begin to visualize a situation, event, or person representing your desire. Imagine projecting this movie from your forehead to the energy ball. See the colorful pictures as vivid and alive. Hear the action while the scene plays itself out to your benefit. Feel that this situation will come to pass at the right moment. Take a deep breath. Blow your vision into the ball to give it even more life. Finally, when you are satisfied that your Reiki ball is programmed, pull it into your chest to absorb the energy. Please take a moment to relax and breathe, if you need time to integrate.

Review Questions

1. What is the first step to becoming a powerful healer?

2. What cultures have the tradition of removing malefic energy in their spiritual practices?

3. What are the two different types of Ki?

4. How does a blessing affect our food before consuming it?

5. What is the first body part focused upon in a self-healing session?

Notes

Ch. 4: The Symbolic Level

Reiki level II is the second step on the path of training. By now you already know the theory and practice of working with individuals. The Reiki subjects are physically present with you during the session. You lay hands on the client or yourself. This allows the universal life force to flow through you into another body. Both individuals experience benefit from the session, each person feeling better than before the session began.

The difference between Reiki I and II is the area of emphasis. Working the physical body is the main focus in the first level. Reiki II teaches you how to engage the emotional and psychological aspects of human nature. Karma is also introduced with regard to spiritual advancement. Finally, the practice of absentee healing, or healing a subject from a distance, is presented.

You will also learn about magical healing symbols. Reiki symbols increase the quantity of life energy to areas of the mind and body. They focus this energy like a laser beam to those regions. Reiki symbols are specific to a certain type of healing. They act according to their own nature and direction of the healer. The symbols are a vital part of Reiki practice and, you will learn how to unlock their healing power.

These particular figures are respected and revered among practitioners. It was a common practice to not even reveal the names or designs to the uninitiated. The symbols cannot be employed without the necessary attunements. If any readers are unfamiliar with them, the symbol names are included in the appendix of this book.

Symbols

What exactly is the definition of the word "symbol?" A symbol is a figure that represents a meaning beyond its appearance. It points to a reality greater than the image of itself. For example, the symbol of the Yin/Yang is merely a circle with swirling colors of black and white. It has a drop of black in the white area and white drop in the black section. This is the image that most people perceive, and often it is not given a second thought.

What is the significance of this particular symbol? The Yin/Yang is a Chinese Taoist figure that represents the merging of opposites into a unified whole, the light, male, day, sky, bright elements with the opposite dark, night, female, earth parts of the universe. All are necessary and each contains a little of the other, as indicated by the drops. For example, yin states that men can have feminine attributes like compassion and nurturance. Yang states that females can also have traditional male qualities such as aggressive impulses or violent protective instincts.

A familiar example of a symbol in the West is the cross. The cross is a particular symbol indigenous to several religions. A cross is formed by two lines that intersect, usually halfway in between each line. They are found in several different religions including Christianity, Voodoo, and Celtic paganism. In these contexts, the symbol indicates a meeting between spirit and matter, divinity and humanity. In Christianity, the cross represents the death and resurrection of the God-man, Jesus Christ. Voodoo, an African pagan religion derived from Catholicism, crosses signify the interconnection between the physical and spiritual worlds.

Symbols are also reputed to have inherent power in many religions. Crosses are used to evoke protection and blessings from ordained clergy in Christianity. Catholic priests employ the cross symbol to help perform the healing rite of exorcism. They are used to expel demons from a possessed human being in this manner. Reiki symbols are similar to crosses in that their power can be evoked by those familiar with their mysteries.

There are three magical healing symbols taught in Reiki II. I will refer to them as the power, emotional, and distance symbols. The actual Japanese names for these figures are included in formal Reiki training or in the appendix. I encourage all those not currently Reiki practitioners to take the necessary courses from a qualified Reiki Master. This will allow you to have working knowledge of the symbols. As previously mentioned, one must be attuned to Reiki in order to access their spiritual power.

There are several different ways to invoke the power of the symbols. One means of activating the energy is drawing them by hand. It is a common practice to trace the figures with the palm of the dominant hand. Students who are fairly new to level II training are encouraged to draw the symbols until they are committed to memory. A practitioner visualizes them in their mind using their imagination at that point. This is the primary learning to effectively wield the symbols.

You can also trigger the energy of the symbol by chanting its sacred name. This is not a new concept in comparative studies of spirituality. The powers of divinity are called forth through the chanting of secret names in ceremonial magic. These names have a special power inherent within it. Each power word vibrates within a specific spiritual frequency that affects both the visible and invisible worlds.

This concept is best illustrated by orthodox Hebrew teachings. It is considered blasphemy to verbalize the actual Jewish name for God. If the word is spoken, chaotic events and mayhem could ensue. This action is interpreted as an attempt to invoke and control a divine force.

The Mental/Emotional Symbol

The first Reiki calligraphy is referred to as the mental symbol. It works primarily with subconscious mind, the deeper, less visible element of the Self. The subconscious mind is the driving force for nearly all human behavior. Within this area of the mind, all of your past experiences are contained from current and previous lives. This is the storehouse for both pleasant and unpleasant memories. All of these impressions are alive and recorded in this inner world.

The subconscious mind is similar to a sponge. It absorbs new material from the five senses. Every thought, impression, and recollections becomes part of this storehouse. Every bit of data is processed and integrated into its existing system. This information lies deep within the inner recesses of the mind. Individual memories are even recallable from the subconscious mind through hypnosis, meditation, dream work, and deep relaxation.

It is a psychological truism that self-defeating thoughts breed problematic behavior. One of the healer's tasks is to uncover these underlying mental patterns. Personal healing begins when subconscious contents reach conscious awareness. This material must be seen against the light of reality. When this awareness occurs, old dysfunctional thought patterns can be altered through positive suggestions.

The Reiki mental symbol also works with the negative beliefs of the subconscious mind. In fact, the Japanese translation of the figure is "God and Man." This mental symbol allows the Reiki practitioner to energetically implant suggestions into a client. Of course, these suggestions are positive and designed to restore harmony to the seeker. These thoughts flow from the healer's mind to the subject. The result is an improved outlook on themselves and the universe.

The Power Symbol

The power symbol is another important aspect taught in Reiki II. The literal translation of this calligraph is, "I place all power here and now." Practitioners use the power symbol to magnify the quantity of life energy projected. In other words, it increases the healing energy flowing into a person. The power symbol is also used in passing attunements from teacher to student. This symbol is my favorite of the three characters. It is truly a powerful tool for transformation.

The Distance Symbol

The last figure described in Reiki II is the distance symbol. This figure translated means "No past, no present, no future." Reiki students utilize this symbol to heal across time and space. How would you like to heal someone not physically present? his can be an extremely effective addition to your Reiki practice.

Distance healing is not a new spiritual concept. In fact, it is a well established component of many religions such as Spiritualism. During their healing sessions, spiritualists send love and positive energy to people needing extra spiritual support. Edgar Cayce, the great healer, psychic, and channeler, was also an advocate of distance healing. He channeled various spiritual entities from the unseen world. These spirits assessed and helped people overcome major illnesses, all of which occurred over large distances.

Many Christian congregations employ healing over distances for those suffering from physical infirmities. They utilize this as part of a church service. Sometimes, the group creates a prayer chain with the names of various people in need of prayer. Certain evangelical clergy pray over large boxes containing the names of the needy.

Karma

The distance symbol can also be used to clear karmic issues resulting from past experiences. Karma in Sanskrit means "action." Every thought, intention, and deed produces a spiritual effect in the unseen world. This effect trickles down into the physical realm, the world of form. A simple analogy for this may be the example of a young child throwing a stone in a baby pool. The rock hits the water and creates ripples from its entry to the sides of the container. Once the ripples touch the sides, they slowly return to the point of impact. According to karma, all actions, whether mental or physical, return to the sender in a similar fashion. However, if you punch someone in the eye, you will not necessarily receive a similar blow. The universe may teach the lesson in another way, perhaps one designed for the offender to experience similar pain. The lesson may show the folly of physically harming another human being.

The effects of our will always return back to us. In Wicca, a neo-pagan religion, this is referred to as the three- fold law. The effects of our will return to us with three times the original power. In other words, if you bless others, you will be thrice blessed. If you curse others, you will be thrice cursed. Since the spirit world is not bound by physical time, these effects occur at an indeterminate time.

Karma is a concept that spans across many religions. In the Holy Bible, scriptures that suggest karmic repercussions are numerous. Old Testament writings state "as you sow, so shall you reap" or "those that live by the sword shall die by the sword." These scriptures suggest the existence of a universal system of cause and effect. Karma and reincarnation are speculated to be part of Christian philosophy until the sixth century.

The concept of karma is related to Reiki in an important way. Reiki energy is believed to release karmic debt both through attunements and hands-on healing. This phenomenon typically manifests in one of two ways. One, the Reiki practitioner may be healing several issues within a short period of time. Two, during Reiki energy flow, the feelings associated with these problems dissolves into oblivion. Therefore, the conflicts become not so insurmountable and scary.

Jim Heals Himself with Reiki

Here is an interesting story that illustrates the first category. Jim was an attractive commercial and print model living in New Orleans. He lived in the French Quarter, which is considered by many to be a place of intrigue and unusual energy. Jim was always attracted to the world of mysticism and the occult as a result of being born to hippie parents. However, he never committed himself to any particular system, but still enjoyed dabbling.

Jim became interested in Reiki after seeing a demonstration at a human potential workshop. He studied under a Reiki master in his area, one with whom he trusted. Jim loved Reiki and took advantage of every opportunity to practice on family and friends. However, he had a dark past.

Jim had suffered from physical and sexual abuse as a child. His uncle took advantage of him on many occasions. Since Jim's father had died two years after his birth, his uncle stepped in to take care of Jim's mother.

When Jim became an adult, he attempted to put his past behind him. He took excellent care of his health and physical appearance. A few years later, Jim worked in the modeling industry. After studying Reiki I for six months, Jim believed himself ready for the next step along the path of Reiki. He attended a Reiki II course with a qualified teacher and received the required attunement, but something remarkable changed after the initiation.

The transformation inside of Jim instigated a leap in spiritual maturity. It manifested gradually by unpleasant dreams about events from the past. They were dreams of his childhood trauma that reawakened old feelings of insecurity. He felt something growing within himself, but did not know the nature of the change. After three weeks of horrid memories, he sat by himself and meditated on the past week's mental activity. Jim slowly realized that he was not to blame for the sexual abuse. He never fully realized this before. After years of repressing the abuse, Jim finally released the pain and moved on with his life.

As previously mentioned, the three symbols have various purposes. Many techniques exist to utilize the full extent of their power, but one must be trained in level II to know the required method. Distance healing with the respective symbol can be done in the following way.

Exercise I

First, use your imagination by creating a mental image of the ill person. It is also permissible to obtain a photograph. Place your hands close together with about two inches of space between the palms. Reiki begins to flow into the empty space by placing your palms near each other. You might feel a slight pressure on the palms themselves. If you feel this sensation, continue to separate them further apart. Now, take a few deep, calming breaths as you close your eyes. Ask the individual's higher self for permission to proceed with the healing. This practice is done only when the person cannot communicate their wishes. It's always better to first ask their permission.

When about four inches of space separate the hands, hold the physical picture of the person or imagine the person within the empty space. Visualize the distance symbol over the imagined image or photo between your hands. Feel the healing energy of Reiki flow to the person at their location. You may even feel a psychic connection formed the process. When you intuitively feel the healing process is complete, clear you mind by placing the hands together. You may now consider yourself an experienced distance healer.

Exercise II

Another technique involves using a physical object as a method to focus the mind. Again, either ask permission from the person for the healing or connect with their higher self to seek it. Obtain an object to represent the person like a doll or stuffed animal. In this case, I will use a teddy bear as an example. Imagine that the bear is the one needing healing. It is also important to maintain a relaxed awareness during this process to maintain the connection. Next, scan the body of the bear for areas needing energy. Place your hands on these places. When your intuition gives the signal to stop sending Reiki, clear your mind and withdraw your hands.

Both of these absentee healing methods are powerful means of sending Reiki. It is a good practice to record the time and duration of the session. This is helpful for several reasons. One, by documenting each session, it offers an opportunity to solicit feedback from the recipient. Two, a practitioner can modify the technique of length of treatment based on the outcome.

As previously mentioned, the emotional symbol is a figure useful in changing unwanted thinking and behavior. These habits result from unconscious forces within us. We are driven to depression, addiction, anxiety, and other mental disturbances due to faulty mental programming. This usually occurs through traumatic experiences or negative messages from our environment. However, there is hope. This distance symbol allows the practitioner to program the recipient with helpful positive suggestions for future changes. If you are ready to change people's minds, let's begin.

It is important to determine in which area the client needs help. Are they feeling anxious, depressed, or suffering from low self-esteem? They may also be dealing with other issues like addictions. In order to counteract these feelings, their dysfunctional thoughts must be replaced by healthy life-affirming beliefs. This is not a new concept in positively altering the mind. In fact, it is a common practice in cognitive psychotherapy, an effective means of changing unwanted thought patterns.

The basic theory of cognitive psychotherapy is that thoughts precede feelings. Every feeling internally perceived by a human being is related to a prior thought. Ideas often occur quickly and then vaporize into the internal recesses of the mind. Here is how the whole process works. A thought typically results from an event existing prior to it. The brain interprets the situation in light of past experience and introduces an interpretation. A feeling follows the thought based on the interpretation.

Thoughts are things and have tremendous power. Our minds interpret life events and produces a feeling. The nature of thought forms the basis for the feeling. Self-defeating thoughts tend to create feelings of nervousness, sadness, and resentment. As an example, one might reason, "I'll never be a great Reiki practitioner because it requires a high degree of intuition. After all, I'm a left-brained logical thinker." This thinking can cause feelings of failure and inadequacy. Here is a technique to spiritually heal any such ingrained feelings.

Exercise III

Have the recipient sit or kneel on a secure surface like a chair, sofa, or the floor. Ask them to take several slow, deep breaths while their eyes are closed. Encourage the receiver to keep their energy open by maintaining a positive and curious mental state. Stand or kneel by the recipient and ask your healing guides to facilitate healing of their mind, body, and spirit.

Place both hands on the receiver's head, on the crown. Allow the Reiki energy to flow into the top of the head. First, draw the power symbol over his crown. These large quantities of energy life force energy into the head and establish a powerful connection. Second, trace the emotional symbol in the exact same place. It offers a direct link to his subconscious mind. Next, imagine the power symbol once again on top of the head. Finally, place both hands once again on the crown.

At this point, it is time to reprogram the subconscious mind with positive suggestions for inner transformation. These are based on the needs of the recipient. Let me explain how to do this. First of all, the suggestions must be worded in a specific way. Words of negation such as "not" or "no" should be avoided. For example, "Jim will not drink whiskey anymore." This command is counterproductive because the subconscious mind does not process negative vocabulary. The inner mind will only understand that Jim drinks whiskey.

Words such as "don't" or "can't" should be banned as well. How many times has a parent said to their little boy, "Don't hit your sister?" The young boy does it anyway in many cases. He only processed the information, "Hit your sister" in his subconscious mind. The minds of children are especially ruled by powerful inner influences as manifested by imagination and fantasy. This is the realm of the unconscious mind.

Words that express negative feeling states are also to be avoided. Terms such as "anxiety," "fear," or "pain" are not to be included in the mental dialogue. These words have such significant negative associations that it is not even worth mentioning them. For example, the phrase, "You are free from your fear of spiders" appears to be harmless. However, "fear of spiders" is the message received by the subconscious mind. This phrase may even reinforce an existing phobia.

After you plan the proper suggestions, it is time to implement them. Continue to channel Reiki into the crown. Remain open to any intuitive impressions received during the experience. Mentally say the suggestions within yourself. The statements travel directly into their awareness on a deep level. After the silent commands are transmitted, clear your mind.

It would be wise to have several different statements prepared for specific issues. The following suggestions for the issue of alcoholism are helpful: "I am healthy physically, mentally, and spiritually. Each day in every way, alcohol becomes less appealing to me. You enjoy exercise and fitness more than drinking alcohol." Design these according to the unique needs of the recipient. It may even be beneficial to include a statement about avoiding high risk drinking situations like nightclubs.

The power, mental, and distance symbols can be useful in your meditation practice. They are also wonderful objects of contemplation. By focusing your awareness on the idea conveyed, you internalize the energy of the concept symbolized. How? Christians think about the cross as a sign of sacrifice and divine love. Tarot card enthusiasts meditate upon images of the Major Arcana to better understand and read the cards.

Here is an effective technique to learn the Reiki symbols. Practice imagining and chanting the power, mental, and distance figures with eyes closed twice a day, preferably during the morning and night. Students often find that meditating upon awakening and just before sleeping are optimal times. I find that spending five minutes on each symbol is enough in my Reiki contemplative practice. However, you must decide the appropriate amount of time for yourself. The following spiritual exercise should be attempted after practicing the previous meditation for at least one month.

Exercise IV

Create a dimly lit atmosphere either indoors or wait for the darkness of night. If it is your desire, play a soothing musical selection during this session. Focus your attention on the following by either sitting or lying.

Direct your consciousness to the crown of the head. It might even begin to tingle once you focus on it. Draw the power symbol over the crown using your imagination. Feel the powerful energy surge into the sacred center. Now, picture the mental figure at the same spot. Notice how this changes your psychological state. At this point, imagine the distance symbol displayed on the crown. Feel it change your awareness. Finish the sequence with a final power symbol. Direct your attention now to the rest of the chakra centers: Third eye, throat, heart, solar plexus, sacral, and root. Follow the same procedure, directing all three symbols onto them.

This exercise directs large amounts of Reiki energy to the chakra centers. For many people, it becomes a daily practice and a powerful healing experience.

Review Questions

1. How does Reiki I differ from Reiki II?

2. What is a symbol?

3. How do you invoke the power of Reiki symbols?

4. What are the specific purposes of the mental, power, and distance symbols?

5. What is the definition of "Karma?"

6. How do you use the mental symbol for healing the mind?

Notes

Chapter 5: The Third Teachings

Reiki III is the final step upon the path of Usui Reiki training. This degree bestows the title of Reiki master. This term "Reiki master" does not necessarily refer to an expert in healing. It simply means an instructor of students, a trained teacher. A Reiki master is not necessarily a master of anything in particular.

There is only one traditional symbol taught in learning Reiki level III, the master symbol. It is primarily drawn while passing attunements from master to student. The master symbol can also be traced along one's body to facilitate healing of self or others. The distance symbol looks quite similar to the master symbol so be careful when applying it.

There are optional non-traditional symbols briefly covered in Reiki III. The Tibetan Master Symbol is often used to pass attunements, like the standard symbol. Some students like it because it is easier to draw. The Serpent of Fire is another Tibetan symbol. It is often used in passing attunements, clearing the chakras, and awakening the kundalini energy. The Grounding Symbol, like the previous symbols, is also used to pass attunements. Specifically, this symbol separates the aura of participants and grounds the aspirant at the attunements end. The Antahkarana symbol is another symbol taught in Reiki III. It is used in various spiritual interventions such as clearing chakras, connecting to guides, and contacting the higher self. Finally, the Johrei symbol is considered to be a Tibetan symbol. It is commonly hung on temple walls for attracting peace, protection, and success.

Teaching Reiki

Practitioners receive the blessing of becoming a mentor at level III. Reiki teachers have a great responsibility in teaching this discipline.

Instruction includes the history, tradition, and techniques of the art. This involves more than just imparting theory and abstract ideas. A wise teacher sets an example for his students. This is similar to an Indian guru, a spiritual teacher. A Reiki master models the appropriate attitude, technique, and demeanor of a healer. An effective teacher must introduce Reiki, not simply as a healing method, but a lifestyle.

I usually compare it to being a sponsor in alcoholics anonymous. A sponsor is a person that guides an alcoholic through the 12 steps of Alcoholics Anonymous. The mentor introduces the drinker to the inner workings of a spiritual program to remain sober.

This lifestyle of a healer requires a commitment to teach, heal, and evolve in a conscious way. Reiki teachings helps perpetuate the flow of divine energy into the physical world. The master changes the student through spiritual energy and transforms the universe.

A Reiki master is not only a teacher, but a spiritual assistant. They can offer comfort, hope, and solace to those needing assistance. A master may also give spiritual counseling to his clients and students. This serves a vital function because many are searching for spiritual direction in their lives. It can be a blessing to serve the infinite spirit by helping other people.

Spiritual direction is necessary in performing as a Reiki master. This is important because Reiki encourages spiritual growth in the practitioner. Inner development is not always a pleasant experience. As we learn about ourselves, we face difficult challenges, especially in relation to others. I discovered this for myself through many uncomfortable lessons regarding various relationships.

Discomfort can result from encountering the shadow elements of our personality. The shadow contains all of the hidden and repressed parts of us. These are the ideas, thoughts, and feelings that we consider undesirable. We tend to hide these elements from most people. Spiritual evolution, especially through Reiki, often causes the shadow self to emerge. A close friend once told me that Reiki makes "the light lighter and the dark darker." I have found this to be exceptionally true in my practice. I believe that we must befriend our inner demons. They give us an opportunity to become wise and integrate their power back into ourselves.

Reiki students undergo many changes while embarking on this path of light. One such shift is to become physically sensitive to spirits. I have experienced this myself and witnessed it enough not to doubt it. I clearly heard the voices of the unseen after my first attunement. Originally, they were just fleeting impressions in the darkness of my mind. Afterward, they took on a life of their own.

One of my former students, Amanda, had a similar experience in her spiritual development. Amanda was an Aries woman with a longing to help people. However, she was uncertain about how this need fit into her higher purpose. Amanda studied many healing arts including healing touch, Swedish massage, and Reflexology. It was not until she studied Reiki that her life completely transformed.

I attuned Amanda after a one day introductory course on the fundamentals of Reiki. After the initiation, she opened her eyes and stared into the background of the dimly lit room. This lasted for about two minutes. When I asked her about her mental state, Amanda said she was feeling well, but that something was different than before the attunement. She did not explain anymore, so the class ended.

I received a phone call a week later at work. It was Amanda's voice, and she sounded particularly agitated. Amanda explained that while she was alone, she heard her name spoken. In fact, a voice resonated, "Amanda!" in various areas of the house. Needless to say, she was shaken by the experience and asked for my help.

Amanda had no previous dealings with the paranormal. I explained to her the process of communicating with invisible entities. She was to dialogue with the voices and ask them questions. Amanda questioned the unseen presence about its intentions. She was surprised to discover the beginning of a meaningful dialogue.

She also developed an increased ability to foresee the future. It served her greatly in one specific instance. Amanda had a close friend named Janice who was in an abusive relationship. Janice's boyfriend, Mike, physically beat her on several occasions. Amanda tried to convince her to leave the relationship, but to no avail. One day, while Amanda spoke to Janice on the phone, she envisioned Mike threatening her with a knife. It was a disturbing glimpse into the future. Amanda went straight over to Janice's apartment to tell her about the vision. Janice told her that she planned to break up with Mike later that night. Unfortunately, she did not take Amanda's intuition seriously, and Mike pulled a knife on her. Luckily, she was able to escape the situation and flee to a neighbor's house. It is unfortunate that Janice did not listen to Amanda's inner wisdom.

Remember to allow inspiration to guide your inner wisdom in everyday life. The Usui Master attunement along with regular Reiki practice helps you become closer to Spirit. Much will be revealed to you in this journey with the infinite. However, the process of enlightenment is often progressive, not always sudden. This occurs when the student is ready and willing to be open to such insight.

Your receptivity to spirit is often determined by your rate of vibration. Spiritual activities such as prayer and meditation raise it considerably. There are different methods to become spiritually elevated. It may require a simple change in diet and activity. This may naturally occur with self-transformation in diligent practice of Reiki. Some students simply experience a need for different foods. These foods often carry a different energy, which is more aligned with your new body.

A Spiritual Diet

If you want to raise your vibration by diet, here are some suggestions. One, reduce the consumption of red meat and hooved animals. I am speaking of pork chops, steak, lamb, etc. These are considered low vibrational foods for many reasons. One, red meat is more difficult to digest than other foods. If you do eat red meat, consider eating organic grass fed meat. Free-roaming animals are usually killed humanely. One could also discover the location of the life stock by chatting with your local farmer.

Another dietary recommendation is to reduce poultry such as turkey and chicken. This category is one step away from hooved animals. However, these animals are easier to digest than red meat. Therefore, the body expends less energy, which can then be used for enhancing spiritual awareness.

What exactly should you eat? The optimal foods for raising your vibration are fruits and vegetables. These foods are slight, simple, and easily digestible. Produce does not carry the heavy feeling associated with most foods. Unfortunately, these foods are the ones which can leave you hungry after only a few hours. However, vegetables combined with beans will leave one with a satiated feeling. A spiritual eating plan is best designed with a balance between satisfying the body and the spirit.

Fasting is another method to increase your spiritual vibration and psychic receptivity. The reduction or negation of food in consumption is a part of many religious traditions. Fasting works together with activities such as prayer, meditation, and healing work for spiritual enhancement.

Exercise

Exercise is another natural key to increasing health and natural vibration. Physical activity is helpful in tuning into your body. Working out can help you learn to be conscious of the body's inner workings. You can determine the level of your vibration at different times. As an example, if working out increases your overall energy, the stress of a difficult day's work may lower this energy. It will be much easier to feel a loss of energy and vibration due to your physical activity.

Spirit Drink

Another way to increase your vibration is with a cool spirit beverage. Among some Reiki practitioners, knowledge is passed about a drink that is spiritually invigorating, almost intoxicating. This beverage is sometimes employed to facilitate the attunement process. It can also be used to increase the level of Reiki in your system. Believe me, this drink is much healthier and less expensive than alcohol.

Do you want to learn how to make this wonderful spiritual elixir? First, obtain a gallon of purified bottled water. This can be bought at any grocery store. If you have a water purification system, that is even better. Next, acquire a container with a detachable top. The container should be able to hold at least a quart of liquid.

Pour the purified water into the jug ¾ of the way full. Locate five small quartz crystals for this tincture. Be sure to wash them to eliminate any impurities that may contaminate the drink. The type of crystal is unimportant for this practice: smoky, clear, and rose are all varieties of quartz in this family. Rub your hands together, stimulating the chakras in them. Hold the five stones, hands side by side, in your open palms. Visualize the power symbol over them and feel them charge with Reiki energy. Next, place your hands together and allow Reiki to flow into the stones.

After you are thoroughly satisfied with the charging of the crystals, drop the stones into the container of water. Draw the Usui Master symbol above the liquid followed by the distance, power, and mental symbols. When these figures are transferred into the mixture, place your hands over the water and allow Reiki to flow into it. When Reiki is no longer traveling through your hands, take a deep breath and imagine the color blue. Visualize a blue mist flowing from your mouth and into the water during the exhalation. Next, hold the cup in your left and place your right hand over the solution. The last step is to verbalize a prayer, with eyes closed, cleansing the liquid of all negative energy. I use the following affirmation: "I invoke thee, O spirit of water to receive the divine power of fire. As I drink this water, I shall receive this initiation of fires light. I declare this to be true. In the name of all that is good, so let it be."

After the entire procedure, the mixture often has a slight metallic taste that some students find unpleasant. It would be wise to pour lemon juice into the water before applying the energy. The suggested amount is half a fresh lemon to each 8 ounces of water. This addition greatly improves the taste. The final step is to drink the blessed liquid. You have just completed the water ceremony.

Peter's Water Ceremony

One of the most remarkable experiences with this practice involved a student of mine whom I shall call Peter. We were participating in his Master level course. After I lectured about the ethics of teaching Reiki, it was time for the water ceremony mentioned above. I prepared the water, as previously outlined, except that we passed the cups that the other had charged.

We drank from the containers holding the sacred liquid. It was an exhilarating feeling that I have never been able to reproduce. I felt a rush of energy flow through me. We looked into each other's eyes in amazement, instantly knowing the other's thoughts. He and I felt connected to an infinite source of light and love. After about thirty seconds, I stood up from sitting on a chair and felt dizzy. We smiled and drank the rest of the spiritually charged water.

I have collected data among Master teachers regarding this rite. The effects of the ritual are both reliable and consistent in its effects. In every case, both master and student feel a sense of peacefulness and contentment after drinking the mixture. Typically, the participants perceive an expansive shift in their awareness and describe a light feeling.

The water ceremony increases the force of the Reiki Master attunement. This final initiation into the Reiki mysteries can be powerful. I will not outline the steps to perform attunements in this book. You can obtain a manual from a qualified Reiki Master during a level III course.

The White Light Meditation

In the courses that I teach, a white light meditation follows the water ritual. These two practices work well together to prepare the student for the inevitable master attunement. This particular spiritual exercise is guided by the instructor to enhance the initiation. It is a wonderful experience to feel the tranquility as the energy raises your vibrational level.

In my psychotherapy work, I have also used this meditation to calm the mentally ill and chemically dependent. It is an excellent method for balancing the mind before problem solving. I am about to show you a powerful white light meditation. This exercise can also be recorded to listen to at a later time. The wording is as follows:

"All right, get as comfortable as possible. Close your eyes. Now, take deep, purifying breath. Hold it. Let the breath out slowly and completely. Take another deep breath. Hold it. . . and exhale completely . . . relax every part of your body . . . your toes . . . let go completely . . . your lower legs . . . all the muscles in your lower legs . . . release all tension . . . now, the upper legs . . . and your hips . . . your stomach . . .your chest . . . your back . . . totally relaxed. You are continually aware of everything happening. Relax the muscles in your neck now . . . and your shoulders. . Your arms . . . even into your fingertips. Now, concentrate on relaxing your jaw . . . release all tension from your jaw . . . and the

muscles of your face. You are now experiencing profound physical relaxation from your head to your feet. Let us aim for mental relaxation. In a moment, you will count down from 10 to 1. With each number, you will let go of all worries, anxieties, and sadness. Begin counting. 10, 9, 8, 7, 6, 5, 4, 3, 2, 1. It feels so wonderful to be this deeply relaxed, always in touching with reality. In this mental state, you will do your psychological programming. Repeat the following affirmation seven times:

"IN THE TERRITORY OF THE MIND, THERE ARE NO LIMITATIONS."

It is now time to increase your vibrational rate with feelings of love and positive thoughts. You can do this by surrounding yourself with the protective white light, protecting you from the all harm both seen and unseen. Your mind is only open to suggestions that are helpful and beneficial to you. Bathe yourself in the light. Realize that you are the light. You are not your body, but a being of light. You are an innocent spirit, beyond time and space. Extend your light in all directions . . .into infinity. You are pure love, light, and in tune with the Universe."

The white light meditation and water ritual are complete. Be proud of yourself for successfully navigating through these spiritual exercises. If you are teaching Reiki II students, it is time to attune them. The initiation is usually the most dramatic element of the Reiki class. It is an extraordinary, life-changing experience that most never know.

Violet Breath

The Violet Breath is a spiritual technique for collecting and projecting Ki energy. It is used primarily as a preparatory exercise for passing an attunement. I will briefly mention it and make a suggestion for variations.

1. Inhale a deep cleansing breath.

2. Contract the Hui Yin point (the spot between your anus and genitals) and place your tongue at the roof of your mouth.

3. Imagine a white light traveling down from above and into your crown chakra.

4. Direct it to travel down the front of your body into your dan tien (point between genitals and belly button) and up your body to the center of your head.

5. Visualize this white light turn blue and spin clockwise. Allow it to transform to a violet mist.

6. Visualize the Usui master symbol, while chanting its name. Blow the violet light and symbol into the crown chakra.

7. Release Hui Yin.

If you are not passing an attunement, you can alter number six in a couple ways for healing. One, you may decide to utilize other symbols besides the master symbol. Two, you can direct the symbols and breath to different energy centers. For example, one might work with the mental symbol for psychological healing. You can imagine this symbol with the violet light, then blow it into the crown chakra. Finally, intend the energy to travel into the third eye. If the issue warranted working with deep emotions, then continue to direct the light/symbol into the heart chakra. Your experience and research will decide which symbols and chakras to activate for specific purposes.

Review Questions

1. What is an option if a student cannot pay for their Reiki courses?

2. How can you take advantage of the auditory sense in teaching Reiki?

3. What is the violet breath?

4. What meditation precedes the master attunement? How does it affect you?

5. What purpose does the water ceremony serve?

Notes

Chapter 6: Reiki with Animals

Are you an animal lover? If you have ever owned pets such as a dog, cat, bird, etc., then you know that they are subject to health problems. Some breeds of these species are also prone to specific illnesses. Reiki can be useful in accelerating the healing of our furry or winged friends.

Reiki, like music, can soothe the savage beast. Some animals do not appreciate uninvited touch. You can work in their energy field if this is warranted and safe. If your gentle touch is allowed, the Reiki will promote relaxation and boost their body's natural healing ability. Remember that is always wise to begin practicing animal Reiki with your own pets. If you don't have pets, ask your friends and relatives to spend time with theirs.

An interesting fact about animals is that they also have chakras. These include vertebrates and invertebrates, like snakes, turtles, fish, arachnids, and insects. Their chakras, like humans, can be blocked or disturbed which may cause illness. The role of the pet healer is to positively affect their energy centers to promote wellness.

First, you must determine the health condition, afflicted organ, and any corresponding chakras. If you remember, each chakra governs a specific part of the body. You may also need to research the species anatomy before conducting the healing session. If you do not know the specific illness or its cause, a general healing of all chakras is in order.

If you are a Reiki II practitioner, then you are familiar with the mental, distance, and power symbols. You are going to use these symbols to activate a healing response in the animal. Why not use your hands in all situations? Your subject may be too interested in your hands and even try to lick or peck them.

You will also need to temporarily restrict the animal's movement. Keep it in its kennel, cage, or aquarium. Begin to cleanse the psychic atmosphere in your environment. Invoke the mental symbol and draw it on all sides of the room counterclockwise. When you feel that your environment is pure, draw the power symbol clockwise in every direction. If your surroundings are sufficiently cleansed, then proceed.

The next step is to ground yourself before beginning the healing. If you do not have your own technique, try the following process: Take a few slow deep breaths. After these breaths, inhale once, tense your entire body for two seconds and exhale. Do this at least three times. Imagine that you are a tree with roots traveling deep into the earth. You are strong, centered, and comfortable. Acknowledge that you are here and now fully present in your body.

It is time to begin your healing session with your non-human friend. Call in your healing guides and/or higher power(s) for direction and spiritual assistance. State your intention to provide a healing session for your companion.

Draw the mental symbol in front of you at arm's length. It is better if you can visualize the symbol. Activate the symbol by repeating the name three times. Inhale and grab the symbol in the palm of your right hand. As you exhale, project the symbol with your hand into the 7th chakra. Your eyes and intention ultimately determine its direction. Begin 3 feet away from the animal. Transmit Reiki through your hands into the chakra and through the inner layers of the aura. Intend for the Reiki to balance any disturbed energy in the aura and afflicted chakra. Project Reiki energy until you are intuitively guided to stop.

Each chakra in a human or an animal has a front and back side. Locate the rear chakra chosen to heal your pet. Repeat the same process, but using the power symbol. This adds even more Reiki energy to the healing. Imagine and activate this symbol. Project the power symbol into the back side of the selected chakra. Next, imagine and activate the distance symbol. Project it into the aura and the chosen chakra directing it to heal the condition. Finally, send Reiki energy into this chakra with your hands a couple feet from your subject.

You have utilized all of the Reiki II symbols in the healing session. It is now time to end the session. Be sure to thank all spiritual entities present for their assistance during this process. Verbally acknowledge the end of the healing session such as, "This work is complete!" Clap your hands or ring a bell loudly to dismiss any remaining energies and signify a return to the mundane. If you are inclined, repeat the earlier step to cleanse the room of lingering energies from their aura.

Balancing an Animals Energy with a General Session

We discussed how to use Reiki symbols to treat the chakras and maladies through a healing attunement. What if you choose to approach the illness with a general session? Remember that receptive animals may require less Reiki than humans. Size matters! Allow your intuition to determine the distance in which to project the Reiki energy.

You also approach animals, like humans, in sections. They may become relaxed, lie down, and fall asleep. Allow them plenty of rest and quiet for their recovery. Whether you do the healing attunement or the general session, repeat the process until you observe a positive outcome.

A Knight's Tale

Knight is a seven year old white American Eskimo dog. Autumn, a Reiki master, raised Knight around Reiki since he was a puppy. Unfortunately, Knight has terrible anxiety, especially for strangers visiting his home. Autumn channels Reiki to calm his nerves and make him comfortable around new people. She also applies it to sooth his spirit for visits to the vet, both of which he does not endorse.

Knight contracted a virus one year, which greatly agitated him. He paced around the house, appearing to feel uncomfortable. Autumn placed him beside her in the bed and sent him Reiki energy. He usually does not like sleeping in her bed because he gets hot. However, Knight relaxed, slept through the night and made a quick recovery.

Unseen Animal Helpers

St. Francis of Assisi, the patron saint of animals, is reputed to have communicated with animals during his life. He believed that they were equal to humans in God's creation. Francis even referred to them as "brother" and "sister" in their conversations. If you need help in an animal healing, consider burning a candle and petition St. Francis for wisdom and assistance.

Which spirits may assist with animal healing? One may seek the elementals to assist in the health of your companion. Also, your pet may have an angel or guide acting on his behalf. Discover this information in meditation or through connecting with your pet's psyche. If you know his helpers, ask if information can be revealed about your pet's recovery. Invite them to attend your future healing sessions.

Review Questions

1. What is one effect that Reiki has on animals?

2. What is the procedure for cleansing your environment of psychic impurities?

3. How do you end the healing session with your animal?

4. Who is St. Francis of Assisi?

5. Do animals have chakras?

Notes

_____

_____

_____

_____

_____

_____

_____

_____

_____

_____

_____

_____

_____

_____

_____

_____

_____

Chapter 7: The Practice

TEACHING REIKI

Congratulations on your learning efforts! You are about to learn the methods of the Reiki master, a third degree initiate into the mysteries of Reiki. The question is whether you feel ready to impart your knowledge. Some masters choose not to co-create Reiki practitioners and are content to only share their gift with clients. This chapter is reserved for those who deeply desire to teach this art and are willing to learn its lessons.

Teaching Reiki effectively is an important responsibility among masters. As instructors, we are exemplars for those who wish to acquire our skills.

Investment

How valuable are your Reiki classes? In other words, how much value do your courses add to people's lives? Hopefully, we contribute a significant amount of love and healing to the world. These qualities do not easily translate into monetary value. How does one translate the development of spiritual abilities into a fair price? As an example, the Reiki level I attunement is a process that bestows the gift to the individual. This is not temporary, but a permanent spiritual imprint, a priceless effect.

Money is usually not a pleasant subject to discuss in promoting a Reiki course. Many instructors struggle with this issue. There is a tradition to allow a student to invest in their education. It ensures that they become emotionally bonded to the course work and personally own it. The investment of energy also encourages only the serious students to apply for

Reiki training. Unfortunately, money is the most convenient way of exchanging energy, especially in the world of education.

There is a counter argument to strictly changing a full fee or bartering. What if the student cannot pay the fee? What if they have no visible talent or trade to exchange? Some Reiki trainers use a sliding fee scale which determines the amount of payment based on their income. For example, if a student only earns $10,000 annually, then their level II class may be $25. This system appears to work for many healing schools.

There are alternate means of investing in Reiki training. Some mentors allow students to barter goods and services for their education. As an example, I know of a massage therapist who gave a massage for his level I class. Another student bartered a piece of art, a painted portrait for his loved one. These exchanges are acceptable as long as no one feels cheated. The bartered services should be equitable to the Reiki course.

Let us imagine that a fair price is negotiated. What is an effective way to teach Reiki? The first suggestion is to be flexible in your class agenda. I do not mean allowing the class control of the content of the course. However, make allowances for long breaks to properly renew their energies and allow time to process the information.

One major mistake in communicating and instructing students is self-reference. What I mean is that instructors usually teach according to their own style of learning. Have you ever known a brilliant person who could not teach someone to even boil eggs? They may have the knowledge, but cannot effectively impart it.

I can personally relate to this concept in my own life. My father was an excellent mechanic and loved to repair cars. He seemed to buy defective automobiles just for entertainment. Dad always tried to teach me about fixing cars, but there was something missing. I could only retain small bits of his teachings. We both got frustrated at times.

Needless to say, I could not learn well from his style of instructing. Specifically, he showed me repair work with little explanation.

He was also hesitant to allow me to practice on our vehicle. This later led to an aversion to learning about cars.

My father taught me as his father instructed him years earlier. This was the problem. Humans primarily learn through verbal understanding and practice. I needed not only the visual demonstration, but an auditory explanation and the touch of manipulating the parts. In addition, we achieve mastery by repetition of certain behaviors through trial and error. This is an optimal method of acquiring unlearned skills.

We all process information through our five senses: sight, smell, taste, hearing, and touch. My father only showed me the "how" of mechanics. In other words, he only taught me through my sense of sight. This was not a total waste of time, just incomplete. Do you remember solving math problems on a chalk board? Your teacher probably explained the solution by writing it on the board. This is more effective because she engaged two senses rather than one.

How does this relate to Reiki? The same principle applies to teaching the art of healing. You must capture the senses of your students to help them learn quickly. A mentor of Reiki can appeal to her pupil's vision, hearing, and sense of touch.

Vision is a vitally important sense in Reiki instruction. Of course, this sounds like basic common sense. However, try teaching the hand positions to level I students in a really dark room. They may actually start to question your intentions! On the other hand, an advanced level II class may benefit from a blindfold to learn about sensing energy. This all depends on the student's comfort with the training and their classmates.

Some specific suggestions for organizing your training include writing on a dry erase board. These white boards are usually portable and inexpensive. You can also easily erase any mistakes on its surface. However, the multi-colored markers are the best aspect of dry erase writing. They can add accuracy and depth to your illustrations of Reiki symbols and chakra centers.

Reiki manuals are a "must" for conducting a training class. Most students enjoy reading the history, theory, and application of healing energy. I present written material before attunements in the first phase of a class. Doing this can give you personal time for preparing the initiation process.

Hearing is another important sense in the learning process. Can you imagine learning philosophy or counseling without verbal instructions? This would be quite a difficult task. However, Reiki has both subjects in its healing art. On the other hand, listening is even more important than hearing in learning. A person may hear words, but not pay attention to them.

How can you take advantage of the auditory sense in teaching the art? Be sure to provide a thorough explanation of the history, theory, and practice of Reiki. This may appear to be common sense, but some instructors are not skilled at verbally discussing serious subjects especially healing and spirituality.

Let us assume you are not a skilled public speaker in a classroom setting. What are your options? One idea is to take courses in giving presentations or trainings. These courses are usually taught in community colleges and universities. I took an excellent leisure course at Louisiana State University several years ago. The class taught me about enhancing vocal qualities, improving body language, and preparing for presentations.

Creating an outline is another helpful hint to prepare for your talk. An outline will show the major topics and subsections to be discussed. Outlines can keep your mind flowing in the desired direction. This is especially true for those who become forgetful while speaking.

One final suggestion is to have a few people share the teaching experience. Team teaching is becoming more popular in seminar style education. This style of instruction allows students to learn Reiki from hearing different lecturers. Therefore, a second teacher can enhance the understanding of a greater number of students.

Another instructor can also sit among the students to facilitate the hands-on application of Reiki. In addition, additional teachers can help model the correct hand positions in small group work. A co-trainer can also save you time by helping to perform attunements in large classes. Team teaching is also excellent for minimizing the emotional stress of education.

Touch is the final sense vitally important in teaching healing. In fact, fifty percent of Reiki involves touch therapy. This touch is not like traditional massage. There is no pressure or manipulation of tissue. However, there is a gentle meeting of the body to create a circuit of energy.

Touch is also an important sense on the feeling level. This is a direct experience instead of an objective one. Touch requires intuition rather than analysis. It beckons feeling rather than thought.

There are many terms to describe the sense of touch. Words such as sensing and feeling come close. These words offer linguistic clues to describe a sensory reality that is crucial to teaching and practicing Reiki. This is important to understand because logic and the intellect cannot completely grasp spiritual healing.

How can you effectively use touch to teach Reiki? How about including several experiential activities in the class? Let them experience a personal Reiki session. Perhaps you can balance their energy centers. If not, allow the students to participate in a Reiki share.

I mentioned creating a sphere of Reiki energy in a previous chapter. This Reiki ball is one of my favorite experiential exercises. The activity teaches you to sense energy both intuitively and physically.

The Master level course also offers several experiential activities. This class primarily focuses on ethics and conducting attunements. Learning the process of performing attunements is vitally important to becoming a teacher. The gift of Reiki cannot be passed on without this process.

I teach the attunement process through behavioral training. I do not just tell students the procedure and give them written instructions. "Figure it out yourself" are usually the words of poor teachers. There is nothing wrong with this approach in the right context, but students usually need more training. I typically allow students to practice the symbols on my body as a role play. One can observe their motions through slightly closed eyelids while retaining enough awareness to measure it subjectively.

An amusing exercise is for students to perform attunements by proxy on a large teddy bear, sitting in a chair. A master can fully observe the student trying to activate their paws. Besides, the bears do not mind.

Review Questions

1. What is a fair method of investing in a Reiki class?

2. What is a good technique for teaching Reiki?

3. How can you take advantage of the auditory sense in teaching Reiki?

4. What is the benefit of team teaching?

5. How can you effectively use touch in teaching Reiki?

Notes

Ch. 8: The Practice of Reiki

Have you ever thought about your future Reiki practice? Do you want to heal part time or full time? These are important questions to ponder in your daily meditations. This chapter will discuss tips and suggestions to manifest your goals in Reiki.

Do you have an idea of your future goals with Reiki? Perhaps you want to help an average of four people weekly. You may simply want to develop a full time teaching practice. Let us explore the most common goals and ways to actualize them.

Setting Up a Reiki Practice

One major decision in practicing Reiki is whether to do it full or part-time. Practicing part time definitely has its advantages. You can work full-time in another field and still have time to see clients. This means that you can maintain your financial security without relying on income from teaching or therapy sessions. You are also able to spend more time on family, romantic, or educational pursuits.

Most people perform Reiki on a limited basis for various reasons. They simply choose to not make it a full-time career. This prevents them from feeling the pressures of a Reiki business. The part-time practitioner also has more flexibility to manage other aspects of his life. Some practitioners are pursuing higher education, travel, and other forms of leisure.

Of course, there are some practitioners who welcome doing Reiki full-time. They love spending most of their time sharing their healing and teaching abilities. These individuals usually teach and conduct healing sessions on a regular basis. Their clients are often charged a fee for their services.

I have seen tension existing between these two types of Reiki folk. Some part-time practitioners accuse full-time workers of exploiting Reiki to simply make money. They sometimes deny the validity of "energy exchange" in practice. These students generally do not charge for classes, attunements, or sessions. This is a matter of personal choice.

I usually defend the full-time Reiki practitioner and their willingness to make this commitment. In one sense, they are able to make more of an impact in promoting Reiki. A full- time Reiki healer can spend more time on their craft, and is sincerely motivated to succeed. They also integrate their abilities into all aspects of their life; their livelihood depends on it. Full-time practitioners must also be grounded to handle the challenges of advertising, employees, and finances, the unpleasant parts of a business venture.

Zen in the Art of Advertising

The public must be aware of your talents and gifts to gain business. Advertising is an extremely helpful means to draw attention to your practice. Have you thought about writing an ad for your local New Age or Holistic Healing magazine? Be sure to spread the written word about your healing services. Give yourself credit and recognition as a professional energy worker.

Advertising will probably be your most costly expense. It can also be your most profitable venture. In other words, consider advertising an investment in your Reiki practice. Also, be aware of the venues providing the majority of your clients. In the beginning, I asked local hypnotists, massage therapists, and spiritual readers about the bulk of their business. They told me which newspapers and magazines were the best risk. Another idea is to include a question: "How did you hear about our services?" on your assessment form. This will give you ongoing feedback about your investments.

Writing articles is another valuable method for capturing the public's imagination. The submissions may be in New Age or Holistic Health magazines. Establish your presence in the community. This will also provide an opportunity to display your knowledge about Reiki healing. A second benefit is that your services are usually mentioned at the end of the article.

Employees and Finances

Let us pretend that you set the goal of having a full time Reiki practice. You seriously want to reach people on a large scale basis. Your deepest desires are to write books, produce videos, and teach across the country. These are not lofty wishes, but attainable goals with the right actions.

The business of Reiki can be a time consuming but a rewarding venture. Are you willing to handle all of the work yourself? This is strictly up to you as you consider your personal and emotional resources.

My Reiki practice is currently small because of other personal responsibilities. This is my choice, but it not everyone's path. Since my classes and caseload are small, I do not need extra help. If I decide to expand my practice, I will obtain employees to ensure quality service.

Let us imagine that your practice is growing beyond your control. You also recognize that you need extra help. How will you choose your assistant? Again, I would advise first recruiting former students interested in your field. These people usually have an emotional investment in the work.

Former students are also excellent helpers because they enjoy the Reiki experience. Choose a "Reiki junkie" to assist in your classes. Enlisting enthusiastic people willing to help you organize, plan, and set up your courses will provide a learning experience that reveals another side of Reiki practice. It is often considered an honor to assist the one who taught you Reiki.

Many martial arts studios have a similar business philosophy, especially when students reach Shodan (Black Belt). Black Belts are required to teach a certain amount to advance in degree. This volunteering is a privilege and responsibility to the school.

What if no volunteers exist to help with your practice? You may need to hire a personal assistant. This should be someone with previous knowledge of Reiki and energy healing. The assistant ought to have experience in basic office skills: answering phones, computer work, and basic accounting.

A Reiki Practice Meditation

The following Reiki meditations are excellent for creating a thriving Reiki practice. Meditation I is designed for the beginner, who is unsure about their plans. Meditation II focuses on manifesting ideas already seeded in your mind. Decide for yourself, in consultation with your guides, which meditation is best.

Begin to breathe in and out slowly and deeply. If you practiced the earlier exercises, this should only take between 3-5 minutes. As you breathe, release all tension in your body. Imagine a bright white spiritual light descending from above. Picture it entering your body and nourishing it with a golden protective barrier.

The golden light forms a cocoon around your physical self. The light energy is powerful and loving. Feel yourself ascend above the natural world into a state of timelessness. This is the realm of your guides and teachers.

Feel yourself descend now to a familiar place, a temple of light. As you touch ground, the protective shield of light fades away and disappears. It is no longer needed. Nothing can harm you in this sacred realm.

You are also greeted by a familiar face; one of your spirit guides. She communicates with you telepathically, while leading you into a vast building. Inside you see many beings wearing glowing white robes. They are busy teaching each other about communication with the living, healing from the spirit world, and spiritual advancement.

Next, your guide leads you into a long dim corridor. She explains that you are entering the hallway of your future. You feel yourself enter into your unconscious mind. She tells you, "This is the seat of all your past knowledge and future wisdom. It is also the vehicle for spirit messages from beyond the physical world".

The escort brings you to a large doorway. "This is the Chamber of Dreams", she says. "There is a large television screen hanging on the wall. These are visions of tomorrow seen today. Of course, you must choose the subject."

You pick the topic of your Reiki business. Questions arise in your mind: What type of Reiki practice will bring me the most joy? Which methods can help me financially support myself? What needs to be released from my life to accomplish this goal? Finally, what are the steps to get started?

Notice how your senses swirl just before images appear on the screen. The answers to your questions begin to unfold. Allow the revelations to pour into your conscious mind. Be mindful of all sights and sounds evoked from the television. You can adjust the speed of the film by turning the dials next to it.

Your guide touches you gently signaling an impending departure. As you walk, you realize that you are in front of the temple. Your guide presses his finger on your forehead. You sense a change stirring within you; something special is occurring within you. An awareness is growing. When you become aware of the physical world, this insight is apparent.

Reiki Practice Meditation II

Begin to breathe in and out slowly and deeply. If you practiced the earlier exercises, this should only take between 3-5 minutes. As you breathe, release all tension in your body. Imagine a bright white spiritual light descending from above. Picture it entering your body and nourishing it with a golden protective barrier.

You now have a conscious understanding of your business goals. However, there may be something blocking you from the past. What could it be? Ask your guides and masters for awareness of any obstacles in your path? These could be physical, emotional, or spiritual challenges. When you are finished, clear your mind.

Be aware of any visual or auditory impressions that bubble up. Allow them to freely flow into your conscious mind. When they end, ask one final question: What actions can remove these obstacles for a successful business in Reiki? Now go through the same process again. Finally, imagine the golden bubble fade and disappear around you. You are now safe.

The last step is optional, but helpful for spiritual programming. Keep your eyes closed while maintaining a pleasant sense of relaxation.

Review all of the impressions received during the meditation. Use the information to create pictures in your mind. Create visions of yourself succeeding in the world of Reiki. Make these images bright, vibrant, and close in distance. Feel the power behind these dreams of the future.

Once these visions evoke feelings within you, draw the power symbol into the dominant picture. Notice the symbol transform the future memory. Repeat this process on the minor scenes. Next, draw the distance symbol into the imagery while maintaining the intention to manifest it in the future.

Are you ready for the final step? Send the thoughts into your past using the distance symbol. By using this technique, you are attracting this reality by changing the past. Understand that the subconscious mind does not comprehend time. This is the domain of the conscious mind. In other words, this method convinces it that you have already moved in that direction.

You have done well. Your practice plans have been empowered three fold by influencing the past and future.

Review Questions

1. What are your future goals with Reiki?

2. What must full time Reiki practitioners have to handle the challenge of a Reiki practice venture?

3. What can you do to capture the public's imagination in advertising?

4. What is an amusing exercise for students to practice attuning people to Reiki?

Notes

Chapter 9: The Spirit of Reiki

Reiki Groups

Human beings are embodied on this plane under difficult and stressful conditions. Unfortunately stress can adversely affect us in all areas of life. For example, we may become physically ill due to emotional strain resulting from romantic relationships, work, and family. This strain allows us to become spiritually vulnerable, causing a splitting of the psyche. This mental disturbance can manifest in extreme forms as compulsive gambling, shopping, sex, and substance abuse.

It is vitally important to prevent such conditions by caring for oneself. Self-care is the first lesson in becoming an extraordinary healer; an almost forgotten teaching. Can you imagine honoring the divinity within by refraining from toxic emotions, food, and drugs? People experience maladies of every kind simply by pushing themselves to the breaking point.

These illnesses begin by a small energy imbalance in the aura. Our inner being produces subtle signals indicating a threat to its internal balance. I have outlined exercises for cultivating awareness through meditation and spirit communication in other chapters. The following pages will explain the basics of gathering a group of practitioners for mutual Reiki care. This spiritual support group is known as a Reiki share.

There is nothing more wonderful than exchanging healing energy among Reiki folk. It is an opportunity to experience love, contentment, and fulfillment among kindred spirits. However, I find that it requires a willingness to be open and vulnerable. Extremely independent and self-directed people occasionally experience difficulty in these gatherings.

Fellowship is an added benefit to 21st century Reiki healing groups. There is a unique relationship among those of like mind and similar interests. Many Reiki healers consciously seek self-transformation and service to humanity. Give yourself the experience of participating in these enlightening and heart-warming gatherings with a group of extraordinary people.

Reiki healing gatherings are a product of 20th century practice. Reiki shares consist mostly of those already attuned to the energy. In other words, a reciprocal exchange occurs between practitioners. This does not mean the uninitiated are excluded from invitation. Reiki shares are wonderful opportunity for everyone to experience the light and love of divinity.

You are already working with the Reiki energy and diligently practicing the art. As a solitary practitioner, one may balance their own energy and heal others. If you are a level two or three practitioner, you can even transfer Reiki energy at a distance. What is the next step? Maybe it is time to gather a small team of Reiki healers and spread the positivity.

A Reiki share is a gathering of practitioners in one location for group healing, meditation, and socializing. There are many ways to successfully conduct a "Reiki party." The hosts often lead the meeting focusing on contemplation and energy work. Groups may also flow toward a model of shared responsibility where each participant leads the gathering.

What are some suggested items to successfully conduct a share? A massage table is highly recommended to conduct a group healing. If a subject lies on a floor or sofa, the helpers usually experience knee, back, or neck discomfort trying to treat them. The table allows for several people to lay hands on each person, in turn, while standing. If a participant has a physical limitation, have a chair available to help in comfort. Also, be sure that the spine is straight in any posture. This allows for the energy to flow unimpeded through the body, a common practice in yoga.

Types of Reiki Shares

There are basically two types of Reiki shares: open and closed. The open forum is a blanket invitation for those needing healing. Don't worry! There should be no shortage of people willing to participate. Tell your friends to spread the word about the exciting new healing group. Give them the opportunity to call or email you about further details regarding the event.

Let us assume that several people plan on attending this special occasion. They are probably excited about the opportunity to restore their internal balance and meet new friends. Inviting the actual healers is next on the agenda. This is crucial for several reasons. One, several activities during the share require more than a single practitioner, especially for the hands on healing. Some participants must be skilled in Reiki or another healing art for its overall success. Otherwise, it becomes simply a social gathering for the energetically imbalanced.

The second form of share is the closed group. This is simply a private gathering among friends and relatives. These groups do not tend to grow in numbers, but remain a more intimate gathering. You are unlikely to be invited or hear about the meetings in a closed group session unless you travel in those social circles.

Finding a Reiki Share

Healing shares are becoming more popular due to Reiki's rising popularity. In fact, I have noticed new Reiki magazines and organizations pop up every year. The easier way to find these groups is online. Contact these associations and ask for information about Reiki exchanges in your area. I sought information about Reiki groups in my state a few years ago and discovered most of the organizations extremely helpful.

Hosting your own Reiki Share

Many ideas need to be considered before hosting your healing share. These include such things as advertising, location, guests, equipment, and refreshments. Advertising is an important consideration if you are planning a large event. How about placing an ad in your local newspaper? In fact, most newspapers do not charge for ads placed in the community event section.

Location is important to accommodate the number of guests. Guests are obviously significant in preparing for any party. How many people are you planning to invite? You may not know the exact figure, but it is wise to have an estimate. This helps you understand the dynamics of space, refreshments, and activities needed.

Hotel meeting rooms are an alternate location for the sacred gathering. One benefit is that hotel space can easily accommodate a large number of people. However, administrators do charge a fee for the room rental. If you plan on having consistent Reiki groups, make the hotel administration aware of your plans. A substantial discount is often given for regular events. This also helps build a relationship with the hotel staff, which has added benefits for the future.

The second order of business is to maintain the affordability of your enterprise. Some hosts will ask for a small free will offering during the event to offset the cost of the room. Be sure to communicate this fact when promoting the affair. Most participants are even willing to pay a small fee for the hotel accommodations. Hotels are wonderful to serve the needs of a large number of Reiki partiers.

I hosted Reiki gatherings in both apartments and homes throughout the years. Homes add a warm and comfortable atmosphere that enhances the entire Reiki experience, an informal setting. Most people enjoy sitting on sofas rather than chairs. Remember to consider the total number of participants. Unless you are entertaining a small group, a modest living space may not work.

Equipment

Reiki shares are a type of healing party, a celebration of the life-force. Why not make the event both emotionally and spiritually fulfilling?

I often host Reiki shares for the general public. I attempt to make the meeting space both visually and auditorially appealing. This engages the healers psyche and support the overall healing effect.

Music is a powerful unseen force in our lives, a fundamental aspect of modern existence. Psychologists have well documented that music alters consciousness in human beings. Do you not own music that evokes feelings of sadness, joy, excitement, and peace? We can also use certain feelings to enhance our Reiki gathering.

What particular feeling is best to promote healing? This is important in deciding your choice of music. Most students find that selections designed to promote love and peace increase their flow of Reiki. I believe this to be true in my own practice. Hard rock, rap, R&B, heavy metal, and country are not the best music genres to play during the session (afterward is fine for grounding). Imagine the emotions felt during the listening: anger, lust, sadness, and excitement. Each of them have their proper place, but are time consuming to balance during the actual event. Therefore, I would not recommend any artists not in the classical or new age music field.

Music conducive to Reiki healing is abundant. New age stores often carry specially designed compact disks to enhance the effects of energy work. Many shops employ people knowledgeable in the proper us of music for healing. Some chain stores even allow you to sample the choices before purchase.

The internet is another excellent option to collect healing songs. Many music providers currently charge a fee for downloading songs. You can burn the MP3s on CDs or keep them electronically for future Reiki exchanges. Perhaps you have a friend into New Age music that can burn you selections from their collection of CDs.

Refreshments are another important idea to consider for your Reiki share. Again, guests primarily determine the amount of drinks and snacks. A large gathering requires a greater variety of food and beverages. In case you rent a hotel room, coffee and refreshments can usually be purchased at an additional cost. If you are on a tight budget, ask guests to bring their favorite munchies, pot luck style. This always works and allows everyone an added sense of sharing.

Some guests enjoy bringing alcoholic beverages to the party. I have attended many such gatherings where homemade wine was consumed. Alcohol adds an entirely different atmosphere to Reiki work. I would not advise drinking intoxicating substances before doing a healing activity. There is nothing more distracting than several people laughing and falling out of their chair during an important healing moment.

It is also my experience that alcohol consumption temporarily decreases the flow of healing energy. Alcohol is a toxin to the human body. When people began drinking, Reiki is usually diminished because the energy works to initially balance the centers first. This simply means that the human vessel must increase its vibration for the spiritual energy to pass. This is an example of the spiritually guided wisdom of divine energy.

Now, you have planned the necessary elements of your Reiki gathering. You chose peaceful and harmonious tunes, decided on your guests, and considered some tasty treats. However, there is much more to be done. It is time to contemplate the additional spiritual activities for the sacred gathering.

All of the following spiritual practices seem to be more effective while sitting in a circle. The circle is a symbol for completion, wholeness, and enlightenment. It is also a universal figure of divine protection especially in magical rites. The circle can also represent the soul detached from the earthly plane in metaphysics. In fact, discarnate spirits are often seen in circular form on the physical plane in the form of orbs.

Meditation is a wonderful addition to any Reiki gathering. Many students enjoy meditation at the beginning of the night's activities. People are generally slowing down from their busy day at this time. Their minds and bodies are becoming more relaxed and comfortable. This allows us to better connect with our higher power because less psychic interference exists to interrupt the spiritual reception.

Spiritual energy pours into your being from guides and masters during meditation. These exalted beings can prepare you for this sacred work. Meditation can also help everyone become centered before healing work. This can set a positive tone for the rest of the night.

How about a message service after meditation? A message service is just tuning into any guides, masters, or departed loved ones in the spirit world. Perhaps they wish to impart a few words of wisdom. My friends and I tune into healing guides for guidance into our general health. This can help you understand where to focus attention during the Reiki work. Be sure to offer thanks for their assistance after the messages are received. Your assistants can also offer you insights in developing further healing skills.

I felt that my current healing therapies were incomplete several years ago. This revelation came to me during a Reiki share. My guides suggested that I learn an additional therapeutic modality. A few seconds later, the term "polarity" flashed and faded in my mind's eye. I later conducted some research to discover a course on something called "polarity therapy."The following weekend was my introduction to this healing art.

Distance healing is another spiritual activity often performed before Reiki shares. Ask the guests to bring a picture of someone needing spiritual help. The specific procedures for spiritual treatments are in a previous chapter. First, ask the group to focus healing energy toward the person, animal, or situation. Call in any guides to improve this process. Thank everyone again present for participating in this sacred event.

Reiki shares can be planned simply or extensively depending on your taste. A simple Reiki gathering is a wonderful idea for busy people. This format requires hardly any preparation or investment of time. A simple event may be three people meeting at 7:00pm on Saturday. Participants convene at a home, turn on soothing music, and transmit Reiki into each other. Afterwards, they eat a small snack of crackers and cheese, while discussing the experience. They part company at 8:30pm to enjoy the rest of the night.

A complex Reiki share has more activities and equipment. The latter is an important consideration. Where will the attendees lay while receiving energy? How about a quilt or yoga mat? I prefer the comfort and stability of a massage table. This also allows healers to easily move around the receivers.

Massage tables generally cost between $200-$600. They can be bought online, at massage schools, and some department stores. Be careful buying these items on the internet; there is no means of examining the structure or durability of the table. Let us imagine you want one for your work, but you cannot even afford an inexpensive table. Another option is to use an existing dining or living room table.

Reiki Share Meditation

Are you ready to experience a spiritual healing on the inner planes? Be sure to loosen or remove any restrictive clothing, including shoes and belts. Begin by taking a deep cleansing breath, exhaling slowly and comfortably. Continue the breathing for about three minutes, and imagine yourself becoming deeper relaxed. Now, imagine a bright white light shining down from beginning to end. Notice the beams move up and down the contours of your physical form. Sense the light also traveling within you and nourishing your vital organs and tissues. This communion with the radiance allows you to feel protected, loved, and whole.

As you continue to feel nourished and serene, see the energy envelop you in a protective white bubble of light. This barrier protects you from all forces both visible and invisible that intend you harm. The bubble is now rising upward and moving into the spiritual planes through time and space. Notice yourself begin to descend further and further down until a mysterious mist appears.

The fog lifts to reveal a beautiful building of golden light. It is a radiant light similar to the sun, but it does not hurt your eyes. You walk toward the structure only to be met by a spirit helper. She introduces herself as a healing guide and asks to accompany you on a trail. The being leads you down a winding path to a lush garden. The landscape is breathtaking with several varieties of flowers and a flowing waterfall.

Seven healing entities greet you both at the entrance. They ask you to come within the garden, and simply sit down, close your eyes, and relax. You sense that they are here to strengthen and empower you. Your guide gently touches your shoulder instructing you to sit cross legged. You intuitively sense the group of seven sitting in a circle around you. They speak about you in silent whispers through the language of telepathy.

Allow the subtle healing force continue to balance and expand your physical, emotional, and mental bodies. These seven beings of light also deeply care about your spiritual health. They are here to assist your healing and overall growth. Release all of your inner fear, anger, and sadness into the light.

You begin to feel the energy flow dissipate from the divine beings. Soon your eyes open to discover a bright white iridescent light surrounding you. You sense that it is time for you to leave. Each of the seven beings wish you farewell. The original guide takes your hand, a sign of impending departure. He leads you out of the garden in front of the building, and warmly embraces you. His form disappears into your body upon touch, a final act of healing. Now surround yourself again with the protective light. Feel yourself rise up slowly again through time and space. Descend now, lower and lower into your physical surroundings. Open your eyes refreshed, relaxed, and balanced.

What about lighting? Each group decides for themselves the environmental conditions of each share. Most shares adopt dim lighting rather than standard bright lights. We automatically associate low lighting with rest, relaxation, and unconscious processes. This sensory experience help practitioners go within, release the ego, and embody the experience.

Music is another ingredient to consider in your Reiki share recipe. Again, this is a matter of personal preference, and is not a requirement. The following are some best practices to consider. The music should be relaxing and not increase physiological arousal. If you are a purist Reiki practitioner, imagine listening to formal Japanese music in your healing share. The ultimate criteria should be whether the music creates a calm and serene state in your participants.

Incense is less common in Reiki shares, but it is definitely worthy of a discussion. Burning incense is a traditional practice of most religions. Holy men assert that incense creates an altered state of consciousness advisable for spiritual activities such as meditation and healing. We will cover more about incense in a later chapter.

Where do you find Reiki people?

Where do you find other Reiki folk for shares and discussion? This need not be a difficult task. If you have been attuned to Reiki, then you already have one friend (your Reiki master). Ask them to introduce you to their other students. In fact, they may already organize Reiki events in which you can participate.

What if there are no current Reiki related activities in your area? One can utilize such websites like *meetup.com* to start a Reiki group in your community. Their monthly fees are minimal, and you can request a "love offering" from participants to reimburse you for the membership. You may also consider joining Reiki groups online. However, this venue may be better utilized for an information gathering/discussion type format.

Cakes and Ale (Grounding)

There is one final piece to participating in a successful Reiki share, which is, adding a ritual of enjoying some food and drink after the healing event. Why is this important? Practitioners may feel ungrounded after an hour of healing work, attuning to guides, or magick. Eating and drinking will stimulate your physiology to become alert again.

Another variation to this theme is contained in the ritual of cakes and ale. This rite is included in some neo-pagan religions, like Wicca. Cakes and ale consist of cookies or cakes, like petit fours; the drink is wine, mead, ale, or beer (only a sip). It is one of the last events to occur in a traditional wiccan ceremony.

If you decide to add this rite to your Reiki share, here are a few suggestions. One, the designated leaders or highest ranked practitioners should lead this part of the group share, preferably a male and female. The two sexes can represent different aspects of the universal force. Individuals with the highest rank ought to lead the ceremony as living representatives of Reiki's knowledge.

The rite begins by giving thanks for the gift of Reiki and its transformative power. Set the dish of cookies and wine on a small table. The two participants leading the ceremony ought to stand together in front of the treats. If one of the leaders is Reiki II or higher, then they charge the snacks and wine with the power symbol. If not, they can simply charge the edibles through their hands. The other leader then says, "We bless this food to nourish our bodies just as Reiki strengthens our spirit. We give thanks for universal life, love, and healing."

The leaders now embrace each other to signify the merging of the male and female energies. Cakes are passed to each participant and a goblet of wine for all to sip. After everyone has consumed their share, the leaders take the final portion for a special purpose. They offer the cake and ale back to the universe by placing it on the earth.

Service Work

Have you ever used your Reiki skills for service work? The term "service work" is actually a misnomer, because Reiki is about service. A more precise question is, "Have you ever donated your healing talents to an individual, group, or organization without financial reward?" If you are already practicing Reiki, the answer is most likely yes. This section will raise your awareness of opportunities to volunteer.

Service work is the cornerstone of all the helping professions, including formal Reiki practice. The inner spirit of the helper may stalk us to assist others in their journey to wholeness. Many suggest that Reiki is a selfless practice, and its servants are spiritually ordained. There are also people initiated into Reiki level I who never heal and do not progress further. Working with these healing energies is not for everyone.

When do we first learn to share? We are initially taught by our parents, grandparents, or other relatives. It is later demonstrated and expressed through other relationships, like friends and lovers. Thus begins our service to humanity, albeit with those closest to us. We usually evolve past our small circle of service and enter into larger social systems. Don't you return energy back to your neighborhood, city, or country?

A Reiki practitioner must decide for themselves their level of service. Does this mean offering Reiki classes *pro bono*? A teacher could acquire many students this way. The early Reiki masters asked their students to invest money in their classes. The field has now become more flexible about this practice.

A student can also offer their healing services for free by request through an email list. One can set aside a couple hours to send Reiki non-locally to acquaintances across the world. If you enjoy more face to face contact, allow time each week to meet privately with clients.

Another idea is to organize a group of Reiki practitioners and focus all energy on a client through your email list. This "meeting of minds" can even concentrate their healing attention on a global issue resulting from disharmony, like poverty or animal cruelty. The power of a healing group is far greater than the individual. I can attest to this as a leader of many healing and meditation groups.

Demonstrations

Demonstrations are an easy way to spread the art of healing. They allow you to give an introduction to the Reiki mysteries. Most people have absolutely no knowledge about this subject. You may be their first living image of a Reiki healer. Be sure to make a lasting impression.

I have given demonstrations for health centers and wellness fairs. Demos are exciting when your audience is genuinely interested in Reiki. This is usually the case in my experience. Hecklers and cynics seldom appear at these events. A general spirit of goodness and open- mindedness often repels them.

Health centers and wellness fairs are perfect for interacting with the public. It is a safe place for others to learn about healing, without the pressure of a weekend commitment. Demos are also a wonderful way to advertise your Reiki practice. People are generally curious about energy work, and enjoy live events. Furthermore, demos can be an exciting way to exhibit your skills. I am going to reveal my format for demonstrations in a moment. Feel free to change it according to audience size, location, and resources.

What day and time is best for your rendezvous? Consider the time periods most likely to get the best response. Demos tend to work best as an evening session on the weekday. Try to avoid Friday or Saturday nights because many people have plans. Also, be leery of Sunday morning demos due to church attendance. Monday through Thursday evenings at 6 or 7pm seem to work for most people.

Let's start with the arrival of the first few guests. First of all, be sure to acknowledge everyone that walks through the door, especially if they come in late. You own the room with this method and allow for interruptions.

Briefly introduce yourself. Ask about how they learned about the demo. Was it a friend, advertisement, family, or sheer coincidence? People can stumble upon Reiki information in rather unusual ways. Next, obtain a sense of their knowledge about energy healing and intuitive guidance. This is the first opportunity to learn about the members of your audience.

Your audience will be gathering information about Reiki and whether you can teach them. These spiritual seekers are looking for clues to your personality, expertise, and patience. Therefore, use the time before and after the demo to connect with them individually. Now let's discuss the actual demo.

The first item on the agenda is simply becoming acquainted with the audience. Introduce yourself by discussing your experience, credentials, and passion for Reiki. Where did you train and with whom? What led you to this healing art? Why is Reiki meaningful to you?

Give a brief explanation of Reiki healing after the introduction. Next, ask for volunteers to participate in a quick session. Allow everyone to have an experience rather than simply an intellectual understanding. The last part should involve answering questions and gathering information for future classes.

How about creating a sign up list for those interested in the next Reiki seminar? Students that submit their names may become your base for future classes. Remember to ask for adequate contact information: Name, address, phone number, email, and social media information (you can put them on your list). They may even be interested in future non-Reiki courses. Perhaps you are developing a class on astrology or meditation.

Let's pretend that you decide to give a brief session to the audience. Enlist your social network of Reiki friends or students to help. This should not be a problem. Reiki draws people to further its cause. Volunteers can participate in the mini share and help answer questions afterwards. They can offer a slightly different perspective than the trainer.

Review Questions

1. What is a Reiki share?

2. What are the two types of Reiki shares? What is the difference?

3. Why is it unwise to consume alcohol at during a Reiki share?

4. What is the benefit of cakes and ale at a Reiki share?

5. What are two venues for demonstrations of Reiki?

Notes

Ch.10: Reiki Magick

We discussed energy and meditation as tools for spiritual development in previous chapters. This section adds an addition to these techniques. Modern day psychology, magick, and ritual give us many insights into the unseen. Yet, these methods and their application are not unique to the Usui system of natural healing. They are designed only to enhance traditional Reiki practice. Let's begin our quest into this fascinating subject.

We should start this chapter by asking a simple question: Why study magick at all? There are several responses to this question. First, one should consider studying magick as an alternate means to satisfy earthly needs for yourself and others. How would you like to learn to increase probabilities and nudge reality in a certain direction? Perhaps you have taken action toward a task or project, exhausted your resources, and need extra help.

Second, magick is both an interesting and challenging path to self-development. It will emotionally and spiritually test your resolve. You will learn from your failures and especially your successes. Either way it will forever alter your reality tunnel.

What is Magick?

Reiki is the channeling of life-force energy for healing purposes. Can it also be used for the sake of energy manifestation? The answer to that question is "yes." Magick is the science and art of causing change in conformity with one's will by utilizing energy. Magick involves using the fundamental building block of the universe, energy, for manifestation. Reiki, like magick, follows natural metaphysical law and progresses along a predictable course.

Magick focuses personal or spiritual energy to fulfill a specific goal. This is not unlike many unseen forces like gravity, magnetism, and electricity. As an example, we use receivers to pick up radio waves for the sake of listening to music. These invisible forces are vital and enrich our daily existence. The spiritual energy of Reiki is also a fundamental aspect of our practice.

How does magick occur? In magical traditions, mental concentration and divine power combine to cause transformation in the spirit world. Magicians focus their minds to create subtle changes in that realm. These deliberate shifts in energy are called thought forms. These invisible energy structures increase the likelihood of life events coursing in a certain direction, all of which are directed by the path of one's intention.

Common Aims of Magick

Another important question must be asked before delving into the unknown. What is the best goal for magick, especially Reiki magick? This is strictly determined by the individual. A certain degree of responsibility is required in energy work. In the Wiccan tradition, one basic ethical principle is upheld: "And ye harm none, do what thou wilt." Any action is permissible as long as no one is injured in any way, including you.

The most common needs in which people use magick are love, prosperity, and protection. I worked at a local metaphysical book store where I first learned about magick. I soon realized that magicians also use magick for revenge, avoiding prison, and causing confusion. These are far from the spiritual ideals of the Reiki system. In fact, the Wiccan rede of "harming none" would not completely encompass the spirit of Reiki. Reiki practice is more inclusive and other-centered than merely personal.

After considering all of these matters, a magical element remains in Reiki practice. It is not simply a gentle healing practice. Reiki requires a magical initiation and instruction in directing energy with thought. These tools can work together in harmony to create tremendous change.

Reiki magick is similar to the goals of high magick. Both art forms involve self-transformation by divine power through ritual. Of course, all strivings for material pleasure are considered secondary to inner spiritual change.

Another connection between Reiki and formal magical practice is the progression through a degree system. According to Reiki tradition, a student can only receive the spiritual gift through an initiation by a fully trained master who is qualified to teach the art. Reiki training teaches sacred techniques that are kept secret from laymen and neophytes. Master level students are asked by their instructor never to reveal the magical symbol or attunements. This practice is thought necessary to preserve sacred teachings. We now have the symbols and processes fully explained in modern books and the internet.

Reiki and magick both attempt to align themselves with higher powers to further the energetic quest. This transformation occurs both internally and in the outer world. This is accomplished through the attunement initiation process. Many masters refer to this effect as nothing less than a miracle. After the attunement event, the healing force is automatically activated, like a switch permanently set to the "on" position whenever the energy is needed.

In esoteric mystical traditions, a student becomes empowered by passing through sequential degrees of advancement. There are also three grades of initiation in the Usui system of natural healing. Each degree allows the student to increase his spiritual abilities. In other words, a third level practitioner channels more energy than a first level student.

The student often becomes sensitive to the subtle working of the unseen world. I've seen this occur in countless students through the years. Some students find this an uncomfortable change because of previous teachings regarding extrasensory powers. However, this side effect is not without its positive side. The spiritual sensitivity can help you become a more effective instrument for healing. This is often a necessary stage for later Reiki practice.

Setting Magical Goals

We should now have a conversation about how to set successful magical goals in Reiki magick. There are several thoughts to consider before indulging in your magical desires.

Egocentrism is a common pitfall in magical practice. Magicians who seek their magical ends without considering the impact on others are capable of great harm. Some magicians only pay lip service to this danger when teaching their students. We will discuss questions to ponder so that you do not descend into this abysmal darkness.

Traditional magick acts as an amplifier that tends to increase the twists or kinks in the human psyche. In other words, it can make one's imperfections even worse. If you were to imagine a garden hose with a tiny leak, more water pressure increases the spilling of water. The once small hole even gets larger through time. Similarly, many magicians, have died penniless with shattered relationships with family and friends. It is unlikely that Reiki magick will lead to such unfortunate events

It is also important to consider both inner and outer ecology when deciding whether it is worth pursuing your goal. Why waste your time using magick or any other method, if your objective will bring you undue hardship. What if you far exceed your goal and got more than you expected? Many imagine themselves winning the lottery. Are you willing to face the consequences of this fulfilled wish? How many stories have you heard about lottery winners spiraling down the path of alcohol, drugs, and poverty?

There are several key questions to check the ecology or integrity of your goals. One, what will happen if you fully and completely receive your wish? Do you imagine an overall positive outcome? Are there some negatives to consider? Is it is worth the effort after a cost benefit analysis? If so, then move forward with your energy manifestation.

Another question is, "What will happen if you don't reach your goal?" Some people perceive a loss of money or health by not acting on their impulse. Might there be a favorable outcome by doing nothing? You may consider forgetting the matter altogether or waiting until a later time to reconsider your options.

A final question to check for ecology is, "How will this affect my environment? In other words, what will be the impact on my health or finances? Will it disrupt my relationships with my family, friends, or reputation in the community? Will it adversely affect my work life?"

Your intent and purpose must also be clear and specific for performing Reiki magick. Where, when, and with whom do you want this to manifest? It is advisable to work out all ambiguities or uncertainties in your mind before conducting your private magical ritual. If your intent is scattered or unfocused, then so will your results. Your wish will not have enough fuel to manifest itself.

One additional suggestion is to frame your desire in a positive way. For example, I once had an acquaintance who said, "I want to make an additional $500 this year." This is much different than "I do not want to be as poor this year." The latter statement is a bit vague. What does poor mean exactly to him? It also declares that which is not desired and uses a pejorative word. This statement will focus the speakers mind on poverty and avoiding it rather than a positive goal to be fulfilled.

You also must avoid certain words in your statement of intent. Avoid "I hope to make an additional $500 in the next twelve months." The word "hope" indicates doubt and assumes the possibility that it won't occur. Also, eliminate the word "try" from you statements of intent such as "I'll try maybe to receive at least $500 extra this year." Your statement must be declarative and confident whether in written or spoken form. Otherwise, the universe may kind of grant it to you maybe.

A final recommendation after constructing your goal is to keep it hidden. There is a maxim in magical work: "To know, to dare, to will, to keep silent."Your magical work should remain a secret to even your closest friends. There is a power inherent in keeping your activities unspoken. If you mention it to your coworkers, family and friends, they may outwardly discourage you or plant seeds of failure in your mind. Loved ones may even do this unintentionally and potentially interfere with the outcome with their own unconscious thought form.

Be sure to offer avenues for the energy to crystallize into your life. If your magical goal is to make yourself more appealing to the opposite sex, you should socialize in various contexts. This is simply following your magical intent with action and allowing it to enter your present reality. If one were to stay home twenty four hours a day, then your chances of meeting a man are slim, unless he is delivering a package.

The Tools of Reiki Magick

Reiki magick uses ritual to increase its degree of success. This includes the use of incense, candles, herbs, and even astrological influences. It may also be necessary to contact advanced life forms like angelic beings. These factors serve to spiritually prepare the practitioner and give extra power for the rite.

The whole concept is similar to cooking a meal. We can make a delicious fancy dinner with many spices and a sauce. It has several ingredients to make it a successful delight. The meal is superior to a ham sandwich in complexity and design. Both meals are edible, but only one will be eaten in a fancy restaurant. Reiki is like this as well. It can be used for magick in its simplest form, but having extra help makes it even more effective.

Reiki energy cannot cause harm, pain, or confusion. In this way, its use in magical practice is narrower than in general magick. For the purposes of this book, these desires center on love, prosperity, healing, and protection. I will provide a short description of magical information in the following page. This is crucial because most Reiki practitioners are not trained magicians.

Before discussing magical implements, I want to pause a moment to consider creating a magical atmosphere. Since rituals were first performed, the ancients observed certain phenomenon about the visible world. The most important of these is that days consist of both darkness and light. Darkness was a reality for the people who fought it with fire and moonlight. Dark energy still holds much mystery in the collective unconscious of human beings.

Consider taking advantage of the dark when conducting magick. It is not surprising that rituals are more effective with the lights dimmed or extinguished. This black cover limits vision and allows you to look within to an inner source of power. Try using the absence of light in your future rituals. This simple technique will enhance your Reiki magick.

Altar

A suitable altar is an important element of all magical practice. An altar is simply a convenient place to lay your ritual implements during a ceremony. This is not only practical, but a practice employed by holy men for thousands of years. Such tools may include candles, incense burners, crystals, and other useful materials.

There are many options to create an altar that is unique to your needs. Some people use an end table, bedroom dresser, or coffee table for their altar. If you have only a few needed implements for the ritual, an end table is an excellent choice. An end table is also easily moved from room to room.

A coffee table is another suitable selection to enhance your rituals and is helpful when the magician needs extra space for his magical tools. If the practitioner plans to conduct rituals in a dining or living room, a solid coffee table would make an excellent altar.

Creating Sacred Space

Before getting into actual ritual items, I'm going to pause briefly and discuss sacred space. When conducting a ritual, certain preparations must occur to set the location apart from the everyday environment. Preliminary practices such as these create a sacred space, a meeting place between the spirit and physical world. This is exemplified in the protective rituals of several religions. As an example, a circle is drawn in several magical traditions to create a boundary between the magical and physical worlds.

The Magick Circle

The circle is one of the oldest symbols of protection known to man. It is without beginning or end and ideal for security from unwanted influences and energies. A protective circle drawn with a focused intent before practicing in any form of magick is highly recommended! A wise Reiki practitioner should conduct all of their magical work within a circle's borders.

How can Reiki students create sacred space? Clergy consecrate salt and water in many religious traditions. Incense is also burned to create a holy place of contemplation, prayer, and worship. These practices can be used to prepare sacred space for Reiki meditation and magick. The following paragraphs introduce some effective practices for establishing a sacred location.

The first step in creating a sacred site for Reiki rituals is to cleanse the area. This requires removing all clutter from the room. Pick up any piles of dirty clothes, boxes, or papers. Clutter attracts negative energy. Those sensitive to energy may notice a slight feeling of heaviness in a messy room.

After straightening up in the chosen location, it is time to actually clean the environment. If you have carpet in your living area, thoroughly vacuuming the floor is essential. However, if you have hardwood floors or tiles, then these surfaces need to be mopped to eliminate all dirt and uncleanliness.

The next step is to cleanse the walls of impurities. This can be done with sea salt water. Sea salt is found in nearly all health food stores and even some grocery stores. Mix a half cup of sea salt to a quarter of purified water. Set the intention to cleanse the water of all impurities from all physical and non-physical sources. Shake the solution thoroughly and place all known Reiki symbols into the mixture. The practice blesses the water and increases the spiritual cleansing power.

The next step is to spiritually exorcise any malefic influences that may be present. First, enter the room and face the north direction. Use a compass if you do not know the direction of north. Draw the mental symbol via your imagination. This symbol is also a cleansing tool. Pivot counter-clockwise to the west and do the same. Continue to move in this direction to the south, east, and back to the north. This practice leaves the room clear of any negative forces.

An alternate method for cleansing your personal ritual space is through herbal incense. In Native American tribes, a smudge stick is burned to sanctify the ritual area. Smudge is usually a bundle of sage and sweet grass. It is also effective for clearing your aura of any negative energy. I have used smudge many times before group meditation sessions.

It helps set the mood for advanced spiritual exercises. Smudge can be found in most herbal stores or bought online.

Additional herbs used for spiritually cleansing of space include frankincense and myrrh. They are not actually herbs, but varieties of gum resin. Frankincense and myrrh are also powerful ingredients used for spiritual purification. The three wise men brought them to Jesus as gifts in the bible. Most Catholic churches still use frankincense during their mass. For our purposes, they can be burned as incense on charcoal blocks or in self-igniting powder.

The third step is to fill the space with a sacred force after cleansing it. Permeate the area with spiritual power. This is similar to the above technique with a different twist. Find the north direction once again. Draw the power symbol with your finger or imagination. This time, pivot clockwise to the right and continue to turn, drawing the symbol until you reach north again. Congratulations! You have just cleansed and charged your sacred space.

Color in Magick

Color is an important element in the practice of magick. Psychologists have long noted that simple colors affect our mood and influence behavior. A house painted bright red is known to create feelings of anxiety and aggressiveness in its occupants. Light blue elicits a sense of peace and tranquility. These effects appear cross culturally in humans, an apparently universal effect.

Color connects us with a specific state of mind, and changes our consciousness to its corresponding theme of reality. Imagine the colors that are in your home. How do they affect you? Take a few minutes to think about this. When you pick out an outfit from your wardrobe, notice how it makes you feel.

Contemplate the answers to these questions at your next meditation session: What predominant colors are in your wardrobe? Why do you suppose that you are attracted to them? Do you have a common color among your other possessions? If so, remember it and how it changes your awareness. This may be your magical power color, which we can be used for influence.

Each color is associated with specific intention in magick. For example, if you wanted to attract prosperity into your life, green or yellow is an excellent choice. This color can be used in various ritual implements such as altar cloths, robes, or stones. However, the most widely used magical item in a magician's toolbox is the candle.

Candle Magick

Candles have been used in ritual for hundreds of years. They seem mysterious to many because of their religious associations. Candles are burned in every major religion including Christianity, Islam, and Buddhism. The former uses them quite frequently, especially in Catholicism. Catholics often burns candles with petitions for healing and other requests.

Candles have no inherent outward power of their own. As in all magical implements, they help focus the human mind. Candles also help us connect to the ancient and powerful parts of our psyche. In this sense, candles become a symbol and catalyst to a deep spiritual power lying within us.

How does one employ candles in magick? The first step is to establish a clear goal for the work. This objective must correspond to the selected color and size of the candle. There is a table in the appendix showing various colors and their correct magical correspondences. Please study this table before proceeding with the next section.

You should have decided on a magical goal at this stage. For the sake of argument, let us say that you want to attract more love into your life. What would be the appropriate candle color(s) for this project? This depends on the nature of the "love" that you seek. Are you attracting a friend or a lover? If you seek a romantic love companion, red and pink are excellent choices. The red suggests a passionate relationship and the pink signifies a heart-felt love.

It is helpful to have your magical goal in written form. This can be done in several different ways. One, you can write the goal directly on a wax taper or votive candle. The statement can be written with a toothpick while you are concentrating on the purpose. In the previous example, the written phrase might be "life mate." Two, it is permissible to write the phrase on a slip of paper and place it on your altar. This phrase should be clear and specific to the desire. After writing your desire on the slip of paper, place it on your altar face up.

Some people prefer to use large candles encased in glass, commonly called seven day candles. I was initially trained in using seven day candles for religious rituals. They are superior for long ritual practices in my opinion. Next, write your chosen phrase on a rectangular piece of paper. After charging the paper, tape the paper against the glass with the writing on the inside. As a reminder, the written desire must contain significant emotional power to be effective.

The affirmation is written on the piece of paper for several reasons. By writing the words, it reinforces the concept in your mind and brings the desire into conscious manifestation. Take a moment and think about this idea for a second. Everything ever created by human beings first began with a simple thought. Art, literature, architecture, and technology started on the inner planes. The concepts preceded their actual form in the physical world.

Another important reason to write the phrase is to mentally create the thought form. It is this collection of mind energy that affects the outside world. By writing the statement, we are also reinforcing its reality in our minds, an investment of mental energy. This is the beginning of its materialization before its physical appearance.

Incense

Incense has been a traditional part of magical and religious practices throughout the world. The peace pipe is used in Native American spirituality to ascend prayers to the gods. Incense is known to create a proper atmosphere for devout prayer and deep meditation. Ancient cultures believed scents could entice benevolent spirits and repel malevolent ones. Although we do not conjure spirits in Reiki Magic, incense adds more power and focus to our intention.

Incense is also used to create an altered state of consciousness in practitioners of neopagan religions. The ingredients, usually herbs, have correspondences to various intents. For example, mandrake root or damiana may be used to attract a romantic partner. Herbs also focus the aspirant's mind in a specific direction toward the fulfillment of the spell.

There are many forms of incense such as self-igniting, cone, stick and loose incense (burned on charcoal). The cone and stick incense are activated by lighting one end. Self-igniting incense is usually mixed with 2-3 parts of herbs before lighting.

Chanting/Incantations

The following section is optional for working with Reiki Magick. Chanting is the repetition of a word or phrase to attract spiritual power for your magical aims. Chants are also repeated to connect with divinity during meditation in some religious traditions. This practice allows the mind to focus on a specific thought through hearing a sacred sound.

Chanting is useful for attuning yourself to the energy of the Reiki symbols. If you want to invoke power for example, you can repeat the power symbol by slowing toning "*Cho Ku Rei.*"The chant activates the symbol and releases the energy toward your intention. Chanting will also help you embody the sound and develop a relationship with its essence during meditation.

Exercise I: Meditation

Take 10 slow deep breaths...Breathing in and out through your nose...Each breath allows all tension to melt way...Feel all muscles from the top of your head to the bottom of your feet Begin to relax, only as quickly as you sense it moving...(If you do not feel adequately relaxed after ten breaths, repeat the process).

"Begin to mentally call bright white light into yourself... the light of protection, the nourishing illumination of the ultimate reality. Allow it to take surround and embody you. Look inward now and locate the God consciousness at the center of your being. This is the all encompassing ground of existence in which you are a part."

"Continue to breathe slowly and deeply through your nose while focusing your consciousness on this point. Hold this process for several moments. You may notice a rush of energy flowing upward to the top of your head. If this occurs, direct your full attention to your breathing and God center. Allow your awareness to expand naturally and embrace the experience."

You may now use this charged state to begin a magical endeavor. However, one can also use this spiritual energy simply to exude more spiritual power. How influential would you be if you walked into a sales situation? Imagine how attractive your energy will be to others while projecting a magnetic aura!

Exercise II

This exercise is similar to the one described in the chapter "Reiki I." The Reiki ball drill was your first introduction to directing energy to create your desires. We are now adding an extra step to amplify and turbo charge the results.

Begin to slow down your breathing by taking long slow deep breaths. Use the following pattern: Inhale for the count of four, hold for the count of seven, and hold for the count of eight. After about ten exhalations, scan your body for any areas of tension or discomfort. If you are drawn to a particular place, focus all of your attention to the area and hold it, while doing the breathing pattern, until it relaxes.

When your body is completely relaxed from top to bottom, continue to slow down your breathing. Settle into a comfortable and peaceful state. Begin to hold your hands apart like you are holding an imaginary sphere. Channel Reiki through your palms and form an energy ball like in the previous chapter. Maneuver your hands around the energy until you feel its surface pressure.

Raise the energy ball up in front of you slightly above eye level. Allow your inner mind to represent your desire as a clear colorful image in the ball. When the picture is firmly embedded in the energy, take a breath and blow even more power into the image. Let the image come alive with movement and even sound. Next, imagine the power symbol and place it inside the ball. Begin to chant its name; do this three times. Allow the image to disappear. Clap your hands or laugh to shift your state and energy. Announce the end of the rite aloud such as, "This work is complete. So let it be."

Review Questions

1. What is magick?

2. What are the common aims of magick?

3. Give an example of the types of words to avoid in constructing your magical goal.

4. What is the maxim commonly used in magical work?

5. What are two common items used in Reiki magick?

Notes

_____

_____

_____

_____

_____

_____

_____

_____

_____

_____

_____

_____

_____

_____

_____

_____

_____

_____

Ch.11: Advanced Reiki Magick

I have just given an introduction to using spiritual energy to fulfill inner wishes. We also discussed magick in shaping the unseen world. The concepts in the last chapter are useful in performing simple rituals, but it can even be taken a step further. This chapter discusses a powerful device to enhance your Reiki Magick.

It is called an energy square. The square consists of five quartz crystals positioned in a four sided arrangement. I will briefly explain the power of crystals before I discuss the square.

Crystals are a common tool used by magicians due to their inherent power. Each crystal has an intrinsic energy to be tapped for magical purposes. They are traditionally used as talismans to attract a certain situation, like love or abundance. Also, certain stones affect the energy of the wearer in alignment with their purpose. Crystals can be worn as jewelry, commonly in necklace form or carried in a bag or pouch. If you are interested, there are many crystal books available online and a few in your local book store.

Magical stones and crystals can also be integrated in the magick described in the previous chapter. One can program a crystal or stone with a magical intention by holding it in the right hand. The magician raises energy within herself and silently repeats a personal desire. She finally shouts her intention and releases the remaining energy into the stone. This process stacks the power contained in the crystal.

Quartz crystals are known to be conductors of both physical and spiritual energy. Have you ever rubbed two crystals together? They are capable of making a small spark. In fact, some cigarette lighters work by two crystals rubbing together to make the initial flame. Another example would be crystal radio kits? They were simple AM radio receivers powered by a battery and a quartz crystal. These kits were popular thirty years ago, a kind of science game for children.

Clear quartz crystals can even be programmed with a specific magical intention. You can hold the stone in your hand and install an image and feeling into it. One may also hold your right hand over the crystal and speak a statement of intention. A verbal or subvocalized incantation is also permissible in programming crystals.

Crystals are also excellent at transmitting psychic energy. They nurture the human spirit, balance our emotions, and help project our power. Crystals represent the element of earth because they are derived from the soil.

Quartz crystals come in many shapes and sizes. I prefer to use white rather than others in that family, like amethyst, rose, and smoky quartz. White, commonly known as clear quartz, is most receptive to thought and intention. I use them exclusively in my Reiki rituals.

Clear Quartz Locations

One can obtain quartz in many locations around the world. The easiest way to acquire them is online or at a local New Age book store. I have found many extraordinary crystal treasures on the shelves. They may call to you wanting to further your work.

People can actually dig for crystals in caves in many states. I have friends that go to Arkansas regularly for this reason. The land owners often charge the participants by the total weight of the quartz taken from the earth. White quartz is sometimes on the surface to be discovered in places like Sedona, Arizona.

Let's imagine that you have located a supply of clear quartz. How do you choose the ones for Reiki magick? The following technique is superb for making an intuitive decision regarding crystals.

Choosing the Right Crystals

First, set your intention with a question to yourself: What six crystals will be successful in conducting Reiki magick? Repeat this several times before proceeding with the next step. Use your receiving hand (non-dominant hand) to scan the crystals with your palm down. You should feel a pull toward specific crystals. I often sense this as a magnetic attraction, like my hand needs to hold it. Do this until six clear quartz are chosen among them.

Find a flat surface to place the stones: a small table or desk should be sufficient. It is also important for the area to remain undisturbed in your absence. In other words, please take the proper precautions to ensure the sanctity of the area.

Once you find a suitable place for the crystals. Consider laying an altar cloth on the surface beneath them. This is optional and not a requirement, and it will not affect the overall magick effect.

Place four crystals on the cloth in a square pattern. Allow a fifth crystal to lie at the center. Notice that the square and its points consist of four equal triangles. Hold each crystal between your palms and let the energy cleanse them. Do this for the five that make up the square. Exclude the sixth crystal, which is the power crystal. Feel the universal power emanate through your body. Know that the powerful force is correctly charging the precious stones.

Let us focus our attention now on the power stone. This stone is the means by which the five crystals remain charged. Therefore, it is known as the power or master crystal. It accomplishes this by directing psychic energy from the practitioner through the stone into each remaining crystal. If you have performed the previous procedures, then congratulate yourself. You are almost finished a powerful magical act.

The Reiki crystal configuration is in a square shape pattern. This means four sides and four internal triangles when the outer points are connected to the center. The number four is important in magick and manifestation. Four is the number of stability and that which is unchangeable. Many numerologists consider it a perfect number, the foundation of all physical matter. In religion and the occult, four has significant meaning: the four elements, the four seasons, the four suits of the tarot, and the four horseman in the book of Revelations. The Pythagoreans, a group of mystics that believed in the magical power of numbers, thought the number four represented God. Why? If you add four to its preceding digits, the sum is ten, which reduces to one, the number of the universal intelligence.

It is time to fully empower the crystals in the grid. Hold the power crystal in your dominant hand. Call in your healing guides and masters. Pause a moment and allow them to be present. They are interested in helping you succeed in healing and magick. Take a deep breath to center yourself before proceeding. Point the power crystal toward the center stone. Allow the Ki energy to flow charging it with vitality.

Sweep the power stone in a counter clockwise direction from the center to the outside stone. Move the power crystal in a triangular pattern also counter clockwise. This empowers all crystals in the pattern.

The energy square can be a powerful means of creating change in your life and a tool that needs regular maintenance. This means that the energy must be renewed on a regular basis. The grid is similar to a car; a battery will lose its charge if not replenished by the alternator.

I will mention two ways to regenerate the power of the crystals. The first is to simply repeat the above steps daily. You can incorporate this every day practice in a meditation routine, an evening ritual. This appears to be best for the greatest number of students.

Another way to charge the crystal configuration is by using a picture. This may be a photograph or drawing, whatever works best for you. I prefer to use a drawing simply because it carries the energy signature of the artist. It is my experience that this adds an extra connection between the pattern and designer.

Let me take a moment to explain this from the beginning. The photograph or drawing represents the actual grid, a symbol in which to focus your mind. We can empower the crystals because all thought and matter are connected on a fundamental level, even across distances. We are working with the essence to create changes in the crystal form.

The Technique

Begin to carry your master crystal around during your daily activities. Keep it in a purse, wallet, or pocket. However, it should remain on your person at all times. This practice will likely bring you blessings due to the power of its charge. Several friends directly experience the stones bringing them confidence, love, and money.

Find an undisturbed place away from the unwanted attention of others. Briefly close your eyes and meditate. What exactly are you trying to achieve? Lay the picture on a flat surface like a coffee table or desk. Next, hold the power crystal in your dominant hand and envision the distance symbol. Mentally project the figure into the picture and whisper its sacred name. Obtain a spiritual connection with the grid by using the picture. Change the square moving the power stone clockwise until it feels intuitively full of energy. Finally, break the connection by entertaining other thoughts.

Group Healing

I want to revisit a subject that I discussed in an earlier chapter since it does fit in the context of magick. That is, the collective power of the group is more powerful than the individual in advanced magical practice. The idea is well known in medical research on the power of prayer. In fact, prayer groups have some success in healing the ill. Unusual results occur even in double blind studies where the physicians and patients have no knowledge of the spiritual intervention. Such outcomes usually demonstrate a significant decrease in recovery time and death rates among those terminally ill.

I recently joined an event group on a popular social media site dedicated to using healing techniques for a well-known author of magick. His loyal students, friends, and readers rallied together to lend their energetic support for his health. These healers and magicians knew the power of will and energy to create extraordinary changes in reality.

Contacting Divinities

Transmitting Reiki to a higher power is primarily about gratitude. In other words, this is basically a gesture of thanksgiving. What exactly are the things in which you are grateful? The answer to this question is different for each person. Some people are grateful for their health, wealth, and good fortune. Whatever the reason for gratitude, the following pages illustrate an extraordinary way to give back to the universe.

This section is about completing the magic circle, the principle of giving and receiving. A fundamental spiritual law states that we are connected to all aspects of the universe. The Native Americans believed that all existence is united by an intricate web woven by a sacred spider. This web can be considered an energy matrix that joins us physically, emotionally, and spiritually.

Contacting and communicating with divinities is an interesting aspect of Reiki Magick. Many people have specific higher powers in which they like to communicate. Christians typically converse with Jesus Christ in their prayers. Catholics sometimes petition for holy saints to intercede in their time of need. Hindus may speak directly to Ganesha, Shiva, or Shakti. The Kabbalists may transmit energy to the archangels. Basically, the "who" of these powers is simply a matter of comfort and mental attunement.

The first step in transmitting Reiki to the higher forces of nature is establishing a mental connection. This is simply done by allowing your mind to meet the mind of your target. There are quite a few methods to achieve this goal. Active contemplation, a form of meditation, is the primary way of achieving a mental attunement with the being.

It is now time to contact your otherworldly being. First, collect all of the objects and symbols that relate to the energy of this being. These things can be photographs, drawings, and statues. If you are Catholic and choose to send Reiki to Jesus, place a cross in your meditation space, along with a rosary. On the other hand, a Wiccan may have a pentacle handy with a small statue to transmit energy to the Goddess. Be sure to place these articles near you on an altar or in your meditation space.

First close your eyes. Begin to relax yourself by taking some deep breaths and counting backwards from ten to one. Do this for a few minutes. Open your eyes when you discover yourself feeling peaceful and receptive. Look at the objects that you selected. These items can also be held to connect you with their energy. Now close your eyes once again, and call your higher power by name. Imagine this being filling the blackness of your mind. Feel their divine presence.

Begin to sense a connection with this being. State your intention in the silence of your mind. A particular helpful beginning is to express gratitude for their past guidance, wisdom, and favors. In other words, confess your appreciation for their past efforts on your behalf. If you never received help from them, thank them in advance for future blessings.

The next step is to express your desire to send them Reiki energy. Look within yourself for intuitive direction after this affirmation. Did you receive a light joyful feeling? What about a heavy feeling of anxiety? Your mind has an inner sense about whether or not to proceed. Let us imagine that you do receive a green light, then advance to the final step.

This technique is similar to sending Reiki to people who are not present. In fact, you will use the distance symbol with this method. If you remember correctly, this specific symbol sends spiritual energy across time and space. Unfortunately, some people believe their higher power exists out there, somewhere else in the universe. Higher spiritual beings are often thought to exist in eternity rather than bound by physical time. These may be the reasons for the success of this method.

Let us pretend that you are ready to complete this process. Continue to attune yourself to the energy of your higher power. Become enveloped by the experience through imagining them physically, feeling their essence, and invoking their name. Summon intense feelings of love and devotion within you. Feel them grow with passion from your inner self.

Now imagine the power symbol over the image of the being in your mind. See this figure fade and disappear. Visualize the distance symbol over the original image. Begin to send the energy on its way. Redraw the power symbol in its previous place to finish the technique. Finally, clear your mind when you are satisfied with the process.

You have just experienced an important part of Reiki healing. The student of Reiki will reap many benefits with regular practice. I have noticed a drastic change in my life through this simple procedure. You will experience more joy, contentment, and love through circulating the universal light.

Exercise I

We are going to integrate the knowledge learned in previous chapters for this exercise. Be sure to review the previous chapters titled "Reiki I" and "Reiki Magick." You can also look at the appendix at the end of the book for guidance on creating your specific ritual.

1. Create a sound statement of intent.

2. Prepare all of the necessary supplies for your ritual. Obtain the properly colored candles along with the correct incense and place on your altar.

3. Draw a circle of energy around yourself and your altar.

4. Call upon your Reiki guides or other celestial entities to assist in your work.

5. Construct your energy ball with the visualization of your desire. Empower it with breath and enliven it with the power symbol while chanting its name.

6. Announce the end of the rite and banish with laugher or clapping.

Exercise II

If you have been following the book and doing the exercises, then you have some experience working with energy and manifestation. It is the right time to document your first experience in your magical diary. Remember the following:

1. Date your entry at the top of the page.

2. Record your statement of intent.

3. Write your magical procedure step by step.

4. Write any impressions, sensations, or feelings after the practice.

5. Record the result of the outcome. If you are still waiting for evidence, then leave this blank for the moment.

Sample Ritual: Rite of Romance

Let's combine the knowledge in previous chapters to give an example of a basic ritual in Reiki Magick. This is only an example to demonstrate how all the elements are joined together.

Statement of Purpose: It is my will to attract a compatible man/woman for a long term romantic partner.

After considering consequences of receiving desire (ecological checks), magician moves forward with ritual.

Gather the following supplies and place on altar:

1. A red (Lust), pink (Love), and white (Balance) candle.

2. Patchouli incense.

3. Rose Quartz or any other stone associated with love.

Procedure

1. Draw a large magick circle of energy counter clockwise with a wand, athame, or your index finger. The circle should be drawn clockwise. Light candles and burn incense.

2. Request guides, deities, or other non-physical entities to assist in the ritual.

3. Magician sits before altar and slows breathing to enter a light trance. Create energy ball with hands and imagine your desire within it. Blow into the image to give it vitality. Draw the power symbol into the energy ball, if

you are Reiki level II or higher. Use your intuition to determine when it is time to end the visualization.

4. Thank your guides, gods/goddesses, or other entities present for their assistance. Vocalize a brief verbal statement such as "This work is complete. So let it be" to indicate the end of your rite.

5. Ring a bell or laugh as a physical gesture for the denoument.Use your index finger, wand, or athame to open the circle of energy by tracing it backwards. In other words, redraw the circle counter clockwise to negate it.

6. If you are finished your entire work, eat or drink something to ground yourself and congratulate yourself for a successful ritual.

Review Questions

1. What is an energy square?

2. Name three types of quartz crystals.

3. How can one communicate with divinity?

4. How does one banish and dismiss the energies present in a ritual?

5. What is the statement of purpose for the "Rite of Romance"?

Notes

Chapter 12: Spirit Guides

Many Reiki practitioners believe in the existence of healing guides. These entities are non-physical spiritual beings whose purpose is to increase personal health. Healing guides are called various names by their respective religions. According to the Spiritualist tradition, certain spirits improve the physical health of a living being. They send humans therapeutic energy as needed. In addition, they work with an individual's biochemistry to promote health. Such beings are referred to as Doctors of Chemistry.

Healing entities in other Spiritual Traditions

Each person is assigned a specific Doctor of Chemistry from birth. Besides sending healing energy, this guide is capable of communication with psychically sensitive individuals. This communication with the living is taught during training in the higher realms. This entity may also impart important health information during this communication. He might suggest a particular diet or advise them to increase exercise or relaxation.

There are similar discarnate entities responsible for wellness in the Catholic tradition. They are commonly known as saints in these circles. According to Catholic doctrine, God is the source of all spiritual healing. Furthermore, God can work through saints to provide healing from ailments. If a human prays for healing via a specific saint, God may work through this spirit being to provide healing from ailments. Therefore, saints act as intercessors between humans and divinity.

There is a similar concept in the Old Testament and later Hebrew literature. These otherworldly beings are known as angels. The word angel is derived from the Greek word "angelos" meaning messenger. Angels are God's messengers or emissaries in the physical world. These beings have historically offered protection, comfort, and healing during times of crisis.

Each individual angel fulfills a specific function according to its own nature. One particular archangel, Raphael, offers spiritual healing to human beings.

The Hebrew word "Rapha" means divine healer. Raphael is thought to have given Moses a book of herbs to cure illness and heal blindness in the book of Tobias. Raphael, the divine physician, assists humans to heal their body, mind, and spirit. He channels the spiritual remedy for all illness in Christian and Hebrew tradition. Holy men suggest praying to this archangel during sickness for an accelerated recovery.

Reiki guides are a particular classification of healing guide. They are thought to attend every session and assist in transmitting spiritual energy. These spirit helpers also seem to improve the overall functioning of Reiki practitioners. Sensitive Reiki practitioners intuit their presence through their psychic perception.

I will refer to the words "healing guides" or "Reiki guides" in the following pages. The terms are interchangeable in this chapter. In fact, Reiki guides are a specific species of healing guide and not all healing guides are Reiki guides. However, all types of healing guides perform the same overall function. As an example, all guides can funnel energy from the spirit world to accelerate healing of an illness. They also can transmit spiritual wisdom to a psychically sensitive individual.

It is important to understand that an individual can work with a personal healing guide without being a Reiki student. After all, why should Reiki students have all the fun? You may be asking the question: How does one perceive a Reiki guide?

Everyone senses their guides in the manner consistent with their natural psychic abilities. I perceive my Reiki guide as a red pinpoint of light. This is how the spirit introduced him to me. I suffered from a serious depressive episode at one stage of my life. I was despondent and spent time indoors most of the day. One evening, while ruminating on sad events, I observed the red light. After dismissing it as an optical illusion from my clock radio, I noticed that my spirits lifted, and I experienced a feeling of euphoria, along with my hands turning hot. My intuition told me that the Reiki guide improved my mood by working on my auric field.

Here is another personal experience with a Reiki guide. First of all, I meditate regularly for the sake of emotional balance. I saw something unusual one day during a clairvoyant vision. My eyes were closed, and I was alone in my bedroom. I saw two pairs of hands on my body giving me Reiki. There was no physical pressure associated with the touch. These beings were my Reiki spirit helpers offering their services.

Another student told me about an experience with her Reiki guide. Stephanie is an intuitive Reiki practitioner. Most people connect with Reiki guides only after several months of practice. However, Stephanie noticed them fairly early in her development. Unlike many students, she has a different perspective on them. According to Stephanie, her guides actually hold her hands and place them on a client's body. These body placements areas are the ones most in need of healing.

Through years of research, I found out an interesting fact regarding the healing entities of various spiritual traditions. When we are need in need and sincerely ask for assistance, an entity is almost certainly there to help. I've been told that this matter involves openness and receptivity. If an individual asks for help, they are more likely to feel vulnerable. This vulnerability is initially uncomfortable, but necessary to become open and allow their love to permeate.

An Unseen Helping Hand

Here is a personal story that illustrates this principle. While in my senior year of undergraduate studies, I lived off student loans and grants. As many students know, these funds often do not allow for adequate spending money. One day, that October, I felt sad about not having enough money to pay my rent. As I lay in my bed, I felt a small pressure on my arm. When I looked at my left arm, a quarter appeared on the apex. I grabbed the quarter and looked at the top side. The inscription read: "In God We Trust." Shortly thereafter, I received some money and later paid all my bills.

Openness is often a difficult action to integrate into one's life. In many cases, openness must be cultivated. Willfulness and strength are highly valued in Western society. As a result, many people overemphasize force in problem solving. In other words, the more force used to complete a goal, the less likely that it will manifest. This is basically a warning about the danger of overdoing it. It was only when I surrendered to spirit, that a profound message was communicated.

Meeting your Healing Guide

Begin by choosing soothing and relaxing music in which to meditate. This music should have a relatively slow beat. If this is distracting to you, play a recording of the sounds of nature. Now, it is time to begin the exercise.

Sit in a comfortable position on a sofa, chair, or even the floor. It is extremely important to feel physically comfortable. Take several deep breaths, with eyes closed, in through the nose and out through the mouth. Do this for a few minutes and enjoy the experience.

Now, focus your attention toward the crown of the head. Feel it tense and then relax the muscles on top of your head. Send this part of your body loving, caring thoughts. You might feel a tingling sensation on your head. Feel the crown relax once again and work down through the different parts of your body. This includes the face, neck, shoulders, arms, chest, stomach, upper legs, lower legs, and feet. Do this process slowly and with care. Now, focus on all the relaxed muscles throughout your physical form. Feel the depth of the physical relaxation.

Imagine a bright white light flowing down from the heavens. Know that it is present to protect you from all harm both seen and unseen. Feel the light nourish you physically, mentally, and spiritually. See it flow through you in a vibrant manner. Now, imagine yourself on the fifth floor of a building five stories high. It is beautifully decorated and gives you a sense of comfort. You observe an elevator in the distance. Get inside the elevator and push the down button for the first floor. Feel the elevator drift slowly down to the first floor.

There is a door several feet in front of you on the first floor. Walk toward the door and slowly open it. Look closely at the beautiful scenery. It is a beautiful meadow with tall grass and several trees. These trees offer shade and a place to sit. Relax in this special area for several moments. After a few minutes, you look into the distance and see a figure coming toward you. You can sense that this is a special being, a healing guide. As it approaches, converse with this entity. Ask any burning questions. Feel free to request guidance or healing. Stay with this situation as long as necessary.

It is now time to return to a more normal state of awareness. By following the same procedure, you can return to this wonderful place, and visit with a healing guide at any time. Now imagine yourself back in the elevator and rising up five levels. On the fifth floor, see yourself back in the room and remembering the presence of your healing guide. The meditation is complete.

Spirit Journaling

It is a great idea to remember the conversations between you and the guide. People usually forget these important communications. In addition, writing the conversations, insights, and other occurrences during the meditation are helpful. Consider jotting these down in a special journal or notebook. This serves to provide organization and proper recording of the experiences.

A journal documenting communications between healing guides and yourself is important in another way. A guide will occasionally make a personal prophecy about the future. It may involve a warning about a certain stranger or someone who might cause you emotional or physical pain. These revelations, no matter how unusual, deserve to be materialized on paper. If the prophecy is written, it is a matter of record and can be reviewed at a later time.

Journaling is also helpful, not only for communications with guides, but in Reiki healing sessions. Many times people are biased in their evaluations of themselves, especially in healing. Self-doubt may slowly creep in allowing you to dispute significant therapeutic experiences with clients. Journaling can measure personal progress in developing the healing energy within you. This often helps in developing self-confidence and gives you feedback on your learning.

Guided imagery is an excellent means of communicating with healing guides and spirit helpers. However, there are other ways to work with these guides. They include developing psychic abilities, through training, to increase spiritual perception. Another means is calling upon a healing guide during a session for specific help.

Exercise I

Let us try an exercise in contacting and working with Reiki guides. Get into a comfortable position on a sofa, couch, or chair, preferably sitting up rather than lying down. Take several slow deep breaths breathing in through the nose and out through the mouth. Next, scan your body with your mind. Look for any areas of physical tension in your body. If there are any such areas, connect with them and imagine sending those parts loving relaxing energy. When your body and mind are at ease, proceed to the next step.

While sitting comfortably on the sofa, couch, chair, or floor, with eyes closed, focus upon remaining open on all levels: physically, emotionally, and spiritually. Sincerely believe that a Reiki or healing guide will reveal itself to you. This can occur in various forms, but it becomes more obvious with increased openness. You may converse with the guide either mentally or verbally, even if there is still doubt.

It is often helpful to ask for healing of a mental or physical illness. If there are any personal concerns, speak to a guide about it. They may respond to the message giving you support and comfort. Look for subtle cues like body sensations, faint impressions, or fleeting mental images. Be aware of any changes in your energy level. These are a several ways in which Reiki guides communicate and send healing.

It has been my experience that guides hear all requests and work to manifest inner and outer balance. However, the request must be in agreement with the higher self, the wiser, more knowledgeable part of our being. Some petitions for help are not honored for this reason. It may harm us more to receive the request than be denied. If it seems your petitions fall upon deaf ears, consider that life is unraveling according to a greater plan.

Review Questions

1. Who are Reiki guides?

2. Who is a Doctor of Chemistry guide in spiritualism?

3. What is spirit journaling?

4. Who is the archangel responsible for healing?

Notes

Conclusion

You and I have come to the end of this exploration together. I began by introducing Reiki as a system of spiritual healing. We later discussed the different levels of Reiki and its teachings. As you integrated that knowledge, we covered other aspects of Reiki, including teaching, starting a practice, and service work. Finally, we delved briefly into the world of Reiki magick and how to manifest desires with energy.

I want to make a couple final comments on this topic. The magic section of the book is definitely one that requires a bit of care. If you are a beginner, this is definitely the case. Read through these chapters slowly and perform all exercises in their sequential order. Also, a student familiar with magick may find it elementary or even boring. This is to be expected because this book is an overview and not a tome on manifestation or magick.

Remember that it is important to continually practice the exercises in this book. You will gain many new insights and understandings with each iteration of the meditations. Also, practicing the exercises will cognitively wire in the new healing techniques. Please be kind to yourself and practice them only as quickly as they remain fun. Focus on the wonderful experiences awaiting you with these exercises. Imagine that you have been a powerful healer all of your life and are only now awakening to that reality.

This is a book that should be read many times for reinforcement and practice. If you are a seasoned and skilled Reiki practitioner, use this book as a starting point. Develop and experiment with your own techniques. For example, while doing meditations, ask your guides for other healing symbols to supplement your work. The field of Reiki needs more information to enhance its knowledge.

If you are a teaching Reiki master, consider starting a formal internship after the master level certification. There are many practitioners who stop practicing after level three. Their break leaves their understanding at a superficial level without further training. Students learn quickly and effectively through practice and consultation.

I want to also encourage readers to never be satisfied with their current knowledge. Study Reiki under the tutelage of several instructors. Each teacher has different abilities and has subtle nuances to their practice of Reiki. One instructor may be excellent at sensing and scanning energy in the chakras while another might be adept at Reiki magick.

Reiki, like many fields, is evolving and changing into different forms. There was only one form of Reiki three decades ago. Several different forms exist now in 2014 and others are yet to be discovered. Reiki is also being applied to other healing fields, like traditional counseling and past life therapy.

We are still in the kindergarten stage of our spiritual evolution, even though most of humanity believes that we are highly evolved. You are on the cutting edge of healers bringing more light energy into the collective consciousness. It is an understatement that more energy workers are needed to heal and teach their skills to future generations. Yet, you are here reading these words taking the steps to create a more magical future. Congratulate yourself for completing this journey. May we meet in the light!

Q/A Session

1. What is the history of Reiki?

Much of the history of Reiki was discovered through the travels and research by the Reiki master William Rand.

A discussion about the history of Reiki must begin with its patriarch. Mikao Usui was born in 1865 within a small village in Japan. We know that he studied energy work as a young man, a form of Japanese Chi Kung. These practitioners perform spiritual exercises in slow motion for increased health and wellness. Specific breathing techniques are practiced along with meditation to collect and move vital energy.

Usui traveled all over the orient and Europe studying various disciplines including religion, medicine, and psychology. He is believed to have profound psychic abilities and participated in metaphysical groups. Dr. Usui later became a Buddhist monk after studying the teachings of the Buddha. His increased spiritual awareness enhanced his powers of meditation and contemplation and prepared for his next adventure.

Usui traveled to Mt. Kurama in Japan for a twenty one day retreat in 1922. He prayed, chanted, and fasted during this time. He is said to have engaged in a special meditation while sitting under a waterfall and allowing it to flow over him. Tradition states that this practice opens the crown chakra. Dr. Usui then saw a brilliant light that struck him on the crown. This was the first Reiki attunement delivered directly from the higher realms.

Usui began working on his own body after his spiritual transformation on the mountain. He also discovered that, unlike his former energy work, he could heal others without energy depletion. Usui moved to Tokyo a few months later and started a healing organization. He later opened up a treatment clinic and began teaching courses.

Japan was hit by an enormous earthquake in 1923. There were over 140,000 casualties and many left homeless. The demand for Reiki was great at this time. Usui and his students worked tirelessly to help those afflicted. He opened up a much larger clinic two years later to serve the community and began traveling across the country teaching Reiki. Usui taught over two thousand students in the art of Reiki and trained several teachers. He even received an award from the Japanese government for meritorious service.

Dr. Usui transitioned into spirit on March 9, 1926 due to a stroke. Sensei Usui is entombed at the Saihoji Temple in Tokyo. If any readers would like to visit his grave, there is a beautiful memorial stone on it with an inscription about his life and work with Reiki.

After the passing of Usui, J. Ushida became the president of his Reiki organization, the Usui Reiki Ryoho Gakkai. Five presidents have succeeded him leading up to the present. Dr. Chujiro Hayashi, who is often mentioned in Reiki history, formed his own Reiki organization after breaking way from the Gakkai.

This brings us to the teacher that spread Reiki across the globe, including the western hemisphere, Hawayo Takata. Ms. Takata was born on December 24th, 1900 in Hawaii. Her story with Reiki begins after suffering from serious stomach and lung problems. She chose to attend Dr. Hayashi's Reiki clinic for treatment and was healed after four months. She was so impressed that she began studying Reiki with Hayashi. They traveled together in 1937 teaching in Hawaii where she set up a clinic. She later began teaching in the continental United States.

Takata begin teaching the master level of Reiki in the seventies. She charged $10,000 for a weekend course and trained twenty two masters before her passing in 1980. Her succeeding masters began to make Reiki classes more affordable in the eighties. The original purpose of Reiki was to make it available for everyone to learn. Reiki began to spread more quickly throughout the world during this time.

In the nineties, several Reiki masters began to channel different Reiki symbols and techniques in their meditations. These symbols opened up new possibilities to enhance such qualities as creativity, psychic abilities, and peacefulness. The Reiki masters followed their intuitive guidance, tested their symbols, and applied them in their healing. Now humanity has several different forms of Reiki from the evolution of the Usui system.

2. **What is the original Reiki legend?**

The original Reiki story begins in the middle of the nineteenth century. This story still centers around Mikao Usui who was the president of Doshiba University in Kyoto Japan. Usui was also a Christian minister. One day he was asked by one of his students: "How did Jesus heal?" Usui, not having an adequate answer, began to do research.

He asked Christian leaders in Japan about the healing techniques of Jesus. They replied that it was a divine mystery. Usui later spoke with Buddhists in Japan who told him that the teachings were probably lost, but he should seek enlightenment through Buddhism. Usui journeyed to the United States seeking answers. He enrolled in the University of Chicago's Divinity School where he studied comparative religions and eventually earned his Doctor of Theology degree. Usui also learned to read and write in Sanskrit, the sacred language of India and Tibet. Usui never found an answer to the puzzle in America.

Usui returned to Japan and began study Buddhism in a Zen monastery. He found the secret healing formula written in Sanskrit in an old text. Usui now had the information to heal, but not the ability. He meditated for twenty one days on Mt. Kurama and laid out twenty one rocks to gauge the passing of time. Usui was knocked unconscious by a beam of light on the twenty first day. He received the Reiki symbols, their knowledge, and the attunements during his altered state of awareness.

As Usui left Mt. Kurama, he stubbed his toe and tearing the nail. Usui immediately laid his hands on the injury instantly stopping the bleeding and pain. This was the first miracle that revealed the rediscovering of an ancient form of healing. Usui walked to the foot of the mountain and entered an Inn to eat. The inn keeper warned him not to eat a large meal after fasting for so long. Usui defied him and ate without any adverse effects. This was his second miracle of Reiki. The inn keeper was impressed by his digestive feat and asked whether Usui would see his ill daughter. The girl had a swollen face from a toothache lasting three days. Usui laid his hands upon her face and the swelling and pain subsided.

3. What are some of other versions of Reiki? How are they different?

Usui Tibetan Reiki added Tibetan symbols to the Western version of Reiki. The school believes that Reiki originated in Tibet. Arthur Robertson is credited for adding Tibetan information to the original Reiki. It became known as Raku Kei Reiki, otherwise known as Tibetan Reiki or way of the fire dragon.

Karuna, means "compassion action." Karuna® Reiki is a recent healing system organized by Reiki Master, William Rand at the International Center for Reiki Training. Rand states that a group of Usui Reiki Masters channeled several non-traditional symbols in the early nineties. He experimented with these new symbols to determine their inherent power. Rand later gathered all the information and developed the Karuna® Reiki system.

Karuna® Reiki is believed to be the evolution of the Usui System. This Reiki system has two levels and eight symbols that direct energy for one's emotional and mental well being. It evokes stronger healing energies and is better able to quickly address a broader range of problems. Each Karuna® Reiki symbol has a different frequency. These eight symbols can fill one with love, peace, groundedness, expand creativity, manifest goals, improve learning, along with other functions.

Johrei® Reiki, otherwise known as Vajra® Reiki, was discovered by the Reiki master Mokichi Akada in the 1930's. It was introduced in the United States in 1953. "Johrei" means "white light" or "purification of the spirit." This system blends the Usui system with the spiritual practice of Johrei®.

Rainbow Reiki was developed by a German Reiki Master, Walter Lubeck, in 1989. This form of Reiki includes additional symbols, mantras, and techniques not included in the Usui system. Meditation and crystal therapy is included in the Rainbow Reiki curriculum. Rainbow Reiki practitioners, like the other traditions mentioned, consider this art an evolution of the earlier Reiki system. The primary text of this tradition is

Rainbow Reiki: Expanding the Reiki System with Powerful Spiritual Abilities.

The Seichim tradition of energetic healing is also important to mention. Seichim was founded by Patrick Zeigler after traveling to Egypt and receiving an invisible spiritual initiation while meditating in the pyramid of Giza. After Zeigler came back to the United States, he studied Reiki along with Egyptian religion and mysticism.

The term "Seichim" refers to the spiritual life force of the soul in Egyptian mysticism. The primary symbol of Seichim is the symbol of infinity, a sacred dancing pattern of the sufis. The Seichim frequency is described as an energy of love.

Angelic Reiki is a healing system channeled by the archangel Metatron through Kevin Core. This Reiki draws from the Usui and Shamballa lineages. The attunements help practitioners work with those in the angelic realms and establishes a permanent link with them. Angelic Reiki practitioners provide a conduit for the angelic healing energy to the recipient.

Shamballa is a Reiki energy healing system developed by spiritual teacher John Armitage. Mr. Armitage states that he received clairvoyant instructions for the system from the ascended master St. Germain, an Atlantean high priest. Shamballa healing practitioners claim that it is a more direct connection to the divine energy. Practitioners report that Shamballa offers quite an intense healing experience.

Shamballa Reiki is a combination of Usui Reiki and other new age practices. This healing system includes such things as aliens, angels, crystals, and channeling.

4. What is the relationship between Reiki and sexuality?

Anecdotal evidence exists for using energy healing to charge a man or woman's sex organs. Some sexual problems exist due to temporary anxiety and stress. Reiki has the ability to provide gentle relaxation and balance in the mind and body. Also, energy directed toward the root and sacral chakras can increase physical energy in this area. If you have persistent sexual dysfunction, make an appointment with an ob/gyn or urologist to rule out medical causes.

5. What does the research say about Reiki?

The current research says that Reiki is definitely indicated for relaxation and stress reduction. Anecdotal evidence suggests Reiki for some physical ailments. In *Spiritual Healing: Scientific Validation of a Healing Revolution*, Daniel Benor, MD cites a study that suggests a therapeutic effect on conditions such as depression and physical pain. Reiki was also shown to increase hemoglobin levels in participants in other research.

Critics cite the placebo effect for Reiki's apparent medical benefits. However, studies with better controls and design are needed to properly address its efficacy for physical disorders. Longitudal research is also necessary to gain further knowledge about Reiki's role in health care.

6. How might I practice Reiki in a holistic health setting?

Assessment is the first step in practicing Reiki in a clinical setting. A complete assessment should be written and include a client's symptoms and any medical problems. Write notes on any imbalances that you notice in their auric field. If you are working in conjunction with other health care practitioners, there may be a standard assessment form.

I suggest for you to work as part of a clinic with an interdisciplinary team. Seek out an open and communicative work environment with a strong emphasis on patient care. A collection of health care professionals, along with other energy healers, can offer you consultation, supervision, and support, not to mention a wonderful learning experience.

Here is one final piece of advice. Be sure to give full disclosure about your credentials to your clients. If you are not a licensed health care professional (doctor, nurse, chiropractor, etc.), then communicate this fact. There are legal consequences for practicing medicine without a license.

7. What do practitioners say about how the Reiki energy affects them?

Some people claim that Reiki has a positive impact on their physical appearance. Applying Reiki to the face also seems to relax the muscles. This relaxation promotes a youthful look. The Reiki energy also is known to balance energy and increase vitality. Reiki makes a nice addition to a woman's youth maintenance program.

8. What is the relationship between Reiki and psychic abilities?

Attunements can increase psychic abilities in students. The first three chakras receive high concentrations of energy during the process. One may begin to see or hear into invisible levels of reality. These abilities are generally a side effect of the spiritual initiation and not the purpose of the attunement. Their power and duration are dependent on such factors as body chemistry and spiritual development.

9. Should I ask permission before giving Reiki?

It is definitely a wise practice to ask permission before intervening with Reiki energy. Of course, there are exceptions to every rule. For instance, if the person is in a coma and are unable to give consent. If this is the case, appeal to a higher spiritual authority for permission. I know that many practitioners try to align with the client's higher self, guides, or God.

Asking permission is mainly a karmic issue. Since we "reap what we sow," are there karmic consequences for imposing your will without someone's conscious ability to resist? Perhaps. On the other hand, emergency room doctors prolong and save lives every day without their patient's permission. Imagine the thousands of accidents and injuries that render people unconscious. This is a richly debated topic in healing circles. Look within to your own intuitive guidance for these answers.

10. What is the relationship between Reiki and space/time?

Reiki energy is not bound by distance or time. It is non-local in nature and timeless in expression. Reiki level II teaches practitioners to transmit energy without the client present. One can also send Reiki backwards to past unpleasant experiences or forward to influence future outcomes. Attunements can also be transmitted over distance and through time. One popular Reiki teacher even attunes students through DVD videos.

11. What is the relationship between Reiki and magick?

Reiki and magick are both energetic arts. One of the many applications of magick is physical, emotional, or spiritual healing, the purpose of Reiki. Similarly, Reiki, learned in level II, uses the power symbol for manifestation, a common goal of magick. Manifesting desires are also explored in other traditions besides traditional western Reiki.

12. What is the relationship between religion and Reiki?

Reiki is considered a spiritual activity and is not part of any known religion. Some religious practitioners use Reiki in their healing work, but this is as an adjunct spiritual treatment. If you have a minister's credential and conduct regular religious services, then you will be adding something valuable in serving your congregation.

Spiritual healing crosses all religions and occurs in every culture. The power of prayer, some argue a form of energetic healing, is present in all denominations of Christianity. Modern religions such as New Thought, including Unity, Christian Science, and Church of Divine Science emphasize spiritual healing as the cornerstone of their faith. Other religions such as Wicca pray to the gods and goddesses for their favor and cast spells for a quick recovery.

13. Why does the spirit drink taste unusual?

The Reiki spirit drink is empowered with energy from Reiki and the crystals contained within the liquid. It often has a metallic taste. The Reiki energy changes the chemical composition from its previous state. Enjoy this energy-infused beverage because you can't buy it at your local grocery store or farmer's market.

14. After I become a Reiki master, how can I become a more powerful healer?

You can become a more powerful healer by improving receptivity to energy imbalances. Regular meditation can lead to the opening of your psychic abilities to detect energy. Practice and attend events by Reiki organizations. Reiki on a consistent basis will also increase your sensitivity.

If you are interested in enhancing the flow of Reiki, consider receiving attunements after the master level. Attunements serve to cleanse your chakras and other energy bodies. They also tend to increase the amount of Reiki energy projected through the healer. If you are interested in increasing your knowledge base, stay current on Reiki publications, participate in online forums, and view new Reiki instructional videos.

Color Correspondences

Yellow: Intellect, Focus, Memory, Confidence, Charm, Attraction, Creativity, Imagination, Sudden Change, Action

Green: Money, Abundance, Luck, Fertility, Generosity, Wealth, Renewal, Marriage

Blue: Peace, Truth, Healing, the Unconscious, Inspiration, Happiness, Protection

Orange: Attraction, Stimulation, Adaptability, Stimulation, Encouragement, Luck

Black: Discord, Reversing, Uncrossing, Releasing, Repelling Negative Thought Forms

White: Balance, Spiritual Power, Healing, Truth, Wholeness, Purity, Spirituality

Brown: Confusion, Uncertainty, Doubt

Purple: Spiritual Power, Success, Magic, Protection, Wisdom, Divination, Spirit Contact, Psychism

Gray: Neutrality, Cancellation

Silver: Meditation, Psychic Abilities, Removing Negativity, Goddess Powers

Magenta: Spiritual Healing, Exorcism

Indigo: Meditation, Opening Up Third Eye, Balance Karma, Prevention of Gossip

Gold: Male Deity Powers, Intuition, Understanding, Financial Blessings

Red: Passion, Lust, Enthusiasm, Anger, Raw Energy

Incense Correspondences

Love: Patchouli, Apple Blossom, Lavender, Yarrow, Rose, Jasmine, Gardenia, Apple Blossom, Mistletoe, Moonwort, Fern, Honey Suckle, Birch, Marigold, Juniper

Opening Psychic Abilities: Mugwort, Wormwood, Nutmeg, Mimosa, Lotus

Inspiration: Cinquefoil, Clove, Acacia, Rue, Rosemary, Fir, Hazel, Cypress, Rowan, Oak Moss

Banishing: Frankincense, Myrrh, Cedar, Violet, Vervain, St. Johns Wort, Rose, Rue

Good Luck: Mint, Cedar, Rosemary, Vervain, Cypress, Chamomile, Jasmine, bayberry, Violet, Nutmeg, Lotus

Healing: Carnation, Cinnamon, Rosemary, Peppermint, Rowan, Savory, Lotus, Myrrh, Rose, Apple, Laurel, Wild Cherry, Cinquefoil

Purification: Bay Laurel, Frankincense, Myrrh, Rosemary, Pine, Dragons Blood, Cedar, Marjoram, Oak, Peppermint, Valerian, Salt, Burdock, Vervain, Lavender, Basil

Courage: Rosemary, Dragons Blood, Allspice

Meditation: Myrrh, Wisteria, Frankincense, Cinnamon, Angelica, Bay, Nutmeg

Clairvoyance: Lotus, Acacia, Wormwood, Marigold, Mugwort

Spiritual Power: Musk, Cinnamon, Verbena, Holly, Oak, Dragons Blood, Thyme, Carnation

Herb Correspondences

Relaxation: Lavender

Love: Damiana, Lavender, Mandrake Root, Rose, Vervain, Ginger, Lime, Jasmine, Angelica, Mint, Pepper, Apricot, Apple, Catnip

Power: Dragons Blood,

Sexual Attraction: Dragons Blood, Patchouli

Money/Prosperity: Bilberry, Cinnamon, Almond, Ginger, Jasmine, Oak, Sassafras, Elder, Dill, Pine, Vervain, Vetivert, Mint, Clove, Clover

Psychic Development: Mugwort, Lemon, Vervain

Protection: Cinnamon, Vervain, Garlic

Intellect: Peppermint

Healing: Pine, Sandalwood, Spearmint, Willow, Chamomile, Mistletoe, Lavender, Basil, Garlic, Lime, Rosemary, Nettle, Gardenia, Buckeye

Consecration/Purification: Angelica, Chamomile, Honeysuckle, Orange, Vervain, Myrtle, Nutmeg, Frankincense, Myrrh

Crystal Correspondences

Healing: Agate, Amber, Amethyst, Quartz, Diamond, Jade, Jasper, Peridot, Aventurine, Carnelian, Topaz, Sodalite, Sapphire

Love: Agate, Amethyst, Beryl, Emerald, Jade, Malachite, Moonstone, Topaz, Sapphire, Rose Quartz

Prosperity: Bloodstone, Calcite, Coal, Emerald, Jade, Tigers eye, Opal, Olivine, Chryosoprase, Cats eye, Ruby, Salt

Intellect: Fluorite, Sphene, Zircon

Protection: Lava, Jet, Jasper, Agate, Amber, Alum, Citrine, Diamond, Emerald, Flint, Coral, Olivine, Onyx, Obsidian, Topaz, Turquoise, Apache Tear

Psychic Powers: Amethyst, Aquamarine, Beryl, Citrine, Emerald, Holy Stones, Azurite

Courage: Sard, Lapis Lazuli, Aquamarine, Agate, Amethyst, Bloodstone, Diamond, Tourmaline

Luck: Olivine, Opal, Pearl, Aventurine, Sardonyx, Turquoise, Tiger's-Eye, Amber, Alexandrite

Serenity: Obsidian, Sodalite, Calcite, Carnelian, Diamond, Coral, Malachite, Amethyst, Sapphire

Physical Energy/ Strength: Bloodstone, Amber, Diamond, Beryl, Calcite, Sunstone, Rhodochrosite, Agate, Red Tourmaline

Glossary

Absentee Healing- The art of sending Reiki energy without being physically present. This is also referred to as distance healing.

Athame- A ritual knife used in conducting magick.

Aikido- A defensive martial art that employs body throws and joint locks to physically unbalance an adversary and neutralize a potential attack. Many Aikido styles cultivate the internal power of Ki to perfect their physical, emotional, and spiritual lives.

Attunement- A spiritual initiation performed by a Reiki teacher to activate a student's natural innate healing ability.

Chakra- Literally means "wheel" of energy. There are seven traditional chakras that correspond to various parts of the body.

Distance Symbol- A magical figure, learned during Reiki II, designed to transmit Reiki through space and time. This symbol can be used for past, present, and future life work.

Hara- The seat of Ki in the human body; it is physically located slightly below the navel. This is also commonly referred to as the Tan Tien.

Hui Yin- The point between the anus and genitals that is contracted to accumulate the Ki energy.

Ki- The vital energy that animates life.

Kirlian Photography- A technique for photographing the aura, or electromagnetic field around the body.

Magick- The art and science of causing change in conformity with ones will. Magick employs intention and will to create a subtle effect in the unseen realm that results in change in the physical world.

Meridians- The energy pathways described in Chinese medicine. There are twelve meridians, usually named by the ruling organ.

Mental Symbol- A magical figure, learned during Reiki II, designed to facilitate healing through the subconscious mind.

Microcosmic Orbit- Literally translated as "The Great Heavenly Cycle." This is the path of Ki energy that moves from the Hara, Hui Yin, and then encircles the body.

Power Symbol- A healing symbol, used in Reiki II, designed to increase the amount of Reiki during a session.

Reiki- A general term for various styles of healing that utilize the transfer of energy through the hands.

Reiki I- An introductory course where students learn the history, theory, and basic hand positions for the Usui system.

Reiki II- The second course in the Usui System of Natural Healing. This class emphasizes distance healing, treating the subconscious, and increasing the power or Reiki.

Reiki III- The final course in the Usui System of Reiki. These teachings focus upon learning to pass attunements, ethics, and instructing students.

Reiki guides-Spirit assistants that help facilitate Reiki healing.

Reiki share- A healing group where participants take turns applying Reiki to each other.

Spiritualism- A religion based upon the premise of communication between humans and non-physical entities.

Spirit guide- A discarnate entity assigned to assist in your spiritual development.

Tan Tien- Another term for the Hara.

Three Fold Law- The Wiccan principle that thoughts and actions return to their source with three times the force.

Voodoo- An African Caribbean religion that utilizes rituals to commune with spirits and divine the future.

Wicca- A federally recognized neo-pagan religion known for its observance of nature holidays, spell casting, and healing work.

Usui Reiki Symbols

Level I: No symbols taught

Level II:

Power Symbol: Cho Ku Rei (Cho-koo-ray)

Distance Symbol: Hon Sha Ze Sho Nen (Hone-sha-zay-show-nen)

Mental/Emotional Symbol: Sei He Ki (Say-Hay-Key)

Level III:

Master Symbol: Dai Ko Myo (Die-ko-me-oh)

Optional Level III

Serpent of Fire: Nin Giz Zida (nin-geez-zee-da)

Grounding Symbol: Raku (Ra-ku)

Spiritual Organ: Antahkharana (An-ta-ka-ra-na)

White Light: Joh Rei: (Joe-Ray)

Tibetan Master Symbol: Dai Ko Myo or Dai Ko Mio (Die-ko-me-oh)

Bibliography

Benor, Daniel. *Spiritual Healing: Scientific Validation of a Healing Revolution.* Southfield, MI. Vision Publications. 2001

Conway, DJ. *Celtic Magic.* St. Paul, MN, Llewellyn Publications. 1998.

Cunningham, Scott. *Cunningham's Encyclopedia of Crystal, Gem, and Metal Magic.* St. Paul, MN, Llewellyn Publications, 1998.

Eden, Donna. *Energy Medicine.* New York, NY, Penguin Putnam, 1998

Hoobyar,Tom.,Dotz, Tom.,&Sanders,Susan. *NLP: The Essential Guide to Neurolinguistic Programming.* New York, New York. Harper Collins Publishing. 2013

Lubeck, Walter. *The Complete Reiki Handbook: Basic Introduction and Methods of Natural Application A Complete Guide for Reiki Practice.* Twin Lakes, WI. Lotus Press, 1999.

Murray, Steve. *Animal Psychic Communication: Plus Reiki Pet Healing.* Las Vegas, NV. Body and Mind Productions, 2009.

Penczak, Christopher. *Magick of Reiki. St. Paul, MN. Llewellyn, 2004.*

Stein, Diane. *Essential Reiki: A Complete Guide to an Ancient Healing Art.* Freedom, Ca, The Crossing Press Inc, 1995.

Lubeck, Walter, Petter, Frank Arjava, and Rand, William. *The Spirit of Reiki: The Complete Handbook of the Reiki System.* Twin Lakes, WI. Lotus Press, 2001.

Tompkins, John. *Mastering Reiki: A Practicing and Teaching Primer.* St. Paul, MN. Llewellyn, 2002.

Usui, M. and Petter, F. *The Original Reiki Handbook of Dr. Mikao Usui.* Twin Lakes, WI. Lotus Press, 1999.

www.ingramcontent.com/pod-product-compliance
Lightning Source LLC
Chambersburg PA
CBHW060244050426
42448CB00009B/1573